T0328464

Cambridge Elements ≡

Elements in Politics and Society in Southeast Asia
edited by
Edward Aspinall
Australian National University
Meredith L. Weiss
University at Albany, SUNY

FIGHTING ARMED CONFLICTS IN SOUTHEAST ASIA

Ethnicity and Difference

Shane Joshua Barter
Soka University of America

CAMBRIDGE
UNIVERSITY PRESS

CAMBRIDGE
UNIVERSITY PRESS

University Printing House, Cambridge CB2 8BS, United Kingdom

One Liberty Plaza, 20th Floor, New York, NY 10006, USA

477 Williamstown Road, Port Melbourne, VIC 3207, Australia

314–321, 3rd Floor, Plot 3, Splendor Forum, Jasola District Centre, New Delhi – 110025, India

79 Anson Road, #06–04/06, Singapore 079906

Cambridge University Press is part of the University of Cambridge.

It furthers the University's mission by disseminating knowledge in the pursuit of education, learning, and research at the highest international levels of excellence.

www.cambridge.org
Information on this title: www.cambridge.org/9781108722414
DOI: 10.1017/9781108686891

First published 2020

A catalogue record for this publication is available from the British Library.

ISBN 978-1-108-72241-4 Paperback
ISSN 2515-2998 (online)
ISSN 2515-298X (print)

Fighting Armed Conflicts in Southeast Asia

Ethnicity and Difference

Elements in Politics and Society in Southeast Asia

DOI: 10.1017/9781108686891
First published online: October 2020

Shane Joshua Barter
Soka University of America

Author for correspondence: Shane Joshua Barter, sbarter@soka.edu

Abstract: This Element seeks to make sense of Southeast Asia's numerous armed conflicts. It makes four contributions. First, this study provides a typology, distinguishing between revolutionary, secessionist, and communal conflicts. The first two are types of insurgencies, while the latter are ethnic conflicts. Second, this study emphasizes the importance of ethnicity in shaping conflict dynamics. This is true even for revolutionary conflicts, which at first glance may appear unrelated to ethnicity. A third contribution relates to broad conflict trends. Revolutionary and secessionist conflicts feature broad historical arcs, with clear peaks and declines, while communal conflicts occur more sporadically. The fourth contribution ties these points together by focusing on conflict management. Just as ethnicity shapes conflicts, ethnic leaders and traditions can also promote peace. Cultural mechanisms are especially important for managing communal conflicts, the lone type not declining in Southeast Asia.

Keywords: Southeast Asia, civil war, insurgency, revolution, ethnic conflict, secessionism, communal conflict, peacebuilding

ISBNs: 9781108722414 (PB), 9781108686891 (OC)
ISSNs: 2515-2998 (online), 2515-298X (print)

Contents

1 Introduction

One of Southeast Asia's most striking features is its incredible diversity. The region features various languages (including the Austronesian languages of maritime countries and the tonal languages of the mainland), writing systems (Roman, Chinese, Arabic, and Pali-based scripts), and religions (with Mahayana and Theravada Buddhist–, Catholic-, Confucian-, and Sunni Muslim–majority countries, plus Hindu, animist, and Protestant minorities). It has varied colonial legacies (Portuguese, Spanish, Dutch, British, French, American, and Japanese colonizers, with Thailand not formally colonized), political systems (absolute monarchy, communist, military, democratic regimes), levels of development (from globalized Singapore and oil-rich Brunei to struggling Laos and Cambodia), scale (Indonesia's 260 million people compared to Brunei's 400,000), and more. Given this immense diversity, it should come as no surprise that Southeast Asia has seen numerous conflicts involving ethnicity and differences in political vision.

This Element seeks to make sense of armed conflicts in Southeast Asia, analyzing different forms of war as well as trends over time. It makes four broad contributions. First, it provides a useful way to approach the region's many violent conflicts, identifying distinct types of revolutionary, secessionist, and communal conflicts. Second, it emphasizes ways that ethnicity shapes conflict dynamics. The importance of ethnic leaders, insecurities, and symbols are clear in secessionist and communal conflicts, but revolutionary conflict also involves ethnic recruitment, grievances, and rivalries. Third, this study identifies broad trends in all three types of armed conflict. Revolutionary and secessionist insurgencies feature distinctive arcs, both declining in recent decades, while communal conflicts are more sporadic. Fourth, tying these contributions together, this study focuses on the importance of ethnicity in peacebuilding efforts. Ethnicity is especially important in managing communal conflicts, the lone form of conflict not clearly declining in Southeast Asia.

1.1 Types of Civil War

This Element offers a framework with which to approach different types of civil wars in Southeast Asia. Three forms of violent armed conflict have, over several decades, taken a horrific toll on the region: revolutionary, secessionist, and communal. Revolutionary conflicts are sometimes referred to as ideological conflicts, standing with secessionist conflicts as forms of insurgency. Meanwhile, secessionist and communal conflicts are forms of ethnic conflict (Fox 2004; Kaufmann 1996; Sambanis 2001). Although not covering all forms of political violence, this threefold categorization helps to make sense of the region's many violent conflicts.

Revolutionary conflicts involve armed rebel groups, usually communists inspired by Marxism, fighting state forces in an effort to capture national power and transform their country. Revolutionaries are motivated in large part by ideology, ideas that reject the status quo and provide alternative social visions. Revolutionary movements typically claim to eschew ethnicity in favor of class, sometimes seeing ethnicity as retrograde (Christie 2001, 201). However, communist rebels in Southeast Asia often recruit from particular ethnic groups, feature ethno-nationalist rhetoric, and face resistance from ethnic minorities. Some of the most powerful communist movements in Asia have come from subjugated and exploited communities, suggesting a need to explore intersections of ethnicity and class to understand communist insurgency.

A second form of conflict is secessionism, in which armed rebel groups fight the state not to capture the capital and country but to control their region in hopes of forming an independent state. Secessionism refers to formal demands of a territorially concentrated minority to leave a country. Secessionism often shifts to become more separatist in nature, with rebels accepting some form of self-government (Wood 1981, 110). Secessionist conflicts are deeply informed by ethnicity, with rebels articulating ethno-nationalist messages, insecurities, and differences with the host state. Secessionist movements see their communities not just as ethnic groups but as distinctive nations demanding self-determination. Just as ethnicity shapes revolutionary struggles, class and material grievances are also important in shaping secessionism. However, in secessionist insurgencies, the dominant form of identification is with the ethnic group, with combatants and supporters seeing themselves as excluded or exploited by the host country (Cederman, Weidmann & Gleditsch 2011). Instead of viewing local elites as exploiting the poor, participants are more likely to see them as fighting to protect their community and preserve its culture.

A third type is communal conflict. While secessionist conflicts involve resistance by territorially concentrated minorities, communal conflicts involve interspersed minorities that live alongside and intermingle with other groups. And while revolutionary and secessionist conflicts see rebels fighting the state as insurgencies, communal conflicts typically feature ethnic groups fighting each other in brief, intense moments of violence. The combatants are usually an assortment of gangs, untrained and loosely organized groups that carry out shocking forms of violence against rival communities (Horowitz 1985). Just because the state is not a primary combatant does not suggest that it is absent, however, as communal conflicts typically overlap with political interests and the state often supports a particular side. Communal conflicts can take many

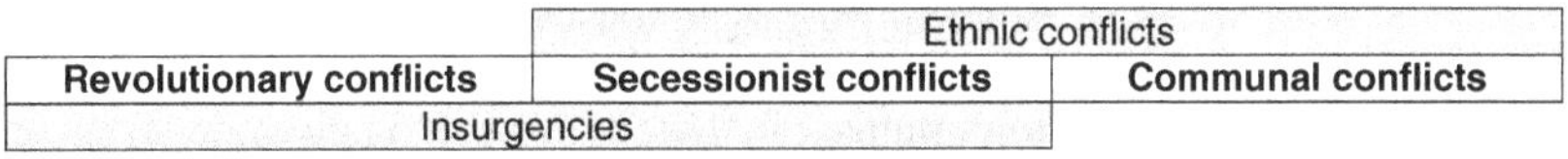

	Ethnic conflicts		
Revolutionary conflicts	**Secessionist conflicts**	**Communal conflicts**
Insurgencies		

Figure 1 Types of civil conflicts

forms, including brief riots, sustained pogroms, and migratory violence, discussed in Section 4. In communal conflicts, ethnic insecurities motivate violence, and groups tend to attack symbolically potent targets. Due to proximity, communities that go to war often have to live beside each other in the aftermath, providing a chronic threat of recurrence.

These three forms of conflict help to make sense of the dozens of armed conflicts across Southeast Asia. The three are laid out in Figure 1, which draws attention to two key factors. Revolutionary and secessionist conflicts are insurgencies, with organized rebel groups conducting guerrilla warfare against the state. In contrast, communal conflicts tend to feature more varied, irregular armed groups, with various gangs clashing with similar groups or unarmed civilians from rival communities. Meanwhile, secessionist and communal conflicts are forms of ethnic conflict, in which sides are most clearly delineated by, and speak in terms of, ethnic identity. These distinctions are blurred in reality, but they nonetheless provide useful indicators to help understand civil wars. This model helps bridge strands of scholarly research on war, as several studies compare revolutionary and secessionist violence as insurgencies (see Mason, Weingarten & Fett 1999) or compare secessionist and communal violence as forms of ethnic conflict (Taras & Ganguly 2015). This study identifies some underlying similarities across these different conflict types but also some important differences, especially in terms of conflict resolution.

At the end of each section, I provide tables summarizing Southeast Asia's revolutionary, secessionist, and communal conflicts. They provide an overview of the cases, identifying the combatants, duration, and casualties of the cases discussed in the respective sections. Casualty data are drawn from prominent armed conflict databases and supplemented with estimates from case experts. These tables are intended to serve as a reference point: casualty estimates provide indicators of the severity of conflicts, but they are subject to considerable uncertainty. This uncertainty is rooted in several factors, including a lack of information, state bias in amplifying or downplaying estimates, the difficulty of knowing whether a given death was due to a given conflict, and the difficulty of separating a particular conflict from other conflicts and events.

1.2 Ethnicity and Civil War

This study emphasizes the importance of ethnicity in shaping all three forms of armed conflict. In emphasizing ethnic factors, it is important to be clear that ethnic traits and differences do not cause violent conflict. Among several scholars studying the link between ethnicity and conflict, Fearon and Laitin (2003, 75) demonstrate that ethnically diverse countries are "no more likely to experience significant civil violence." Sometimes it is easier to manage many groups than a few, and much depends on cross-cutting cleavages (religion, vocation, or political parties may connect groups with different languages or skin colors) as well as the salience of ethnicity in a given society. Ethnic difference is neither a curse nor a problem to be overcome; indeed, the denial of difference is more likely to generate violence than its presence.

The absence of a direct causal link does not mean that ethnicity is unimportant in shaping armed conflict. Scholars disagree on how to measure and assess the relationship between ethnic diversity and armed conflict, but few would suggest that ethnicity is unimportant. Ethnicity influences armed conflicts in numerous ways. Ethnicity can provide a fault line, demarcating sides in war (Horowitz 1985). Although lines are never completely firm (Kalyvas & Kocher 2007), in ethnic conflicts identity shapes allegiance, and individuals cannot easily defect to the other side. Ethnic insecurities can be used by leaders to frame threats and compel action (Brass 1996). Ethnic symbols may encourage violence by providing a sense of meaning, highlighting insecurities, framing various historical lessons, and more (Eck 2009). Ethnic symbols may provide meaning to conflicts, insecurities related to domination, historic lessons, and more (Kaufman 2001). As emphasized in the cases discussed here, ethnicity informs who fights, why they do so, and how conflicts unfold.

Ethnicity is understood as a broad collection of ascribed identity traits. Smith (1996, 445) defines an ethnic community as "a named human population of alleged common ancestry, shared memories and elements of common culture with a link to a specific territory and a measure of solidarity." Ethnicity includes culture, race, language, religion, perceived origins, and a sense of a common future (Kaufman 2001, 16). An ethnic group is different from a nation, a term with a political-economic "edge." Although both are forms of "imagined communities," a nation is typically an ethnic group (although nations may be multiethnic or civic) that sees itself as ruling a specific territory (Anderson 1991). In secessionist conflicts, rebellious minorities typically claim a sense of nationhood, which is not necessarily the case in communal conflicts.

To explain how ethnicity shapes war, experts often speak of primordialism, instrumentalism, and constructivism, even though none of these approaches exist in pure forms (Cederman 2002). We must avoid caricatures and instead speak of tendencies. Primordialism emphasizes that ethnicity is deeply rooted in psychology and history. In this view, ethnicity is "sticky" – difficult to manipulate and changing slowly. Instrumentalism prioritizes how leaders interpret and shape ethnic traits to suit new contexts. This can involve stoking fears about rival groups or elevating ethnic symbols. Constructivism points out that, although appearing timeless, ethnic identities are often quite recent, shaped by elites or changing contexts. All three of these approaches to understanding how ethnicity shapes conflict feature shortcomings and some blind spots. Primordialist approaches must explain change over time and the timing of hostilities; instrumentalist approaches must explain why masses follow leaders to war; and constructivist approaches must keep in mind that the ingredients of new recastings are not simply invented (Chandra 2012).

An emphasis on ethnicity need not come at the expense of other factors. Ethnicity hardly explains when violence takes place. Crises, regime changes, and other structural factors better explain when armed conflicts occur (Bertrand 2004). Material grievances play important roles in motivating struggles, with intersections of ethnic difference and material grievance informing many armed conflicts. Just as revolutionary insurgencies feature ethnic dimensions, ethnic conflicts typically feature a sense of exploitation and exclusion of the weak at the hands of those in power. Horowitz (1985, 22) refers to "ranked ethnic groups," suggesting we might expect especially potent conflicts when "ethnic groups are ordered in a hierarchy, with one superordinate and another subordinate." Focusing on the myriad roles of ethnicity in armed conflicts does not represent a primordialist position or deny the importance of other factors. As this Element suggests, ethnic traits intertwine with material power and class interests in driving war.

1.3 Conflict Trends

A third contribution of this Element is to identify broad conflict trends in Southeast Asia. By analyzing armed conflicts in terms of revolutionary, secessionist, and communal struggles, we can identify broad patterns in the growth and decline of each type. Based on the casualty estimates listed in tables at the end of each section, I show that revolutionary and secessionist insurgencies demonstrate clear arcs that diminish over time. Revolutionary conflicts originated early in the Cold War era, mostly in the 1950s and 1960s, but declined from the late 1970s and the 1980s. This said, revolutionary conflicts have enduring legacies, as Vietnam and Laos feature sustained communist party rule, Cambodia is ruled by former communists, and the Philippines endures sustained revolutionary violence. Meanwhile, secessionist conflicts developed in two groups: the aftermath of colonial rule in the early 1950s; and in response to centralized host states in the 1970s. Secessionist conflicts declined in the 2000s, although not as sharply as revolutionary conflicts, with several cases continuing into the 2020s. Secessionist conflicts have not been overcome as definitively as revolutionary conflicts – they are fading but without a definitive end. Finally, communal conflicts feature distinctive temporal patterns. Instead of existing as a sort of phase particular to specific decades, communal conflicts are chronic, unfolding in times of crisis such as regime change or economic collapse. This means that, even as insurgencies are overcome, communal conflicts represent a constant threat in Southeast Asia, an observation that should inform peace work.

1.4 Conflict Management

The aforementioned contributions – the three types of armed conflict, the importance of ethnicity, and broader conflict trends – come together in Section 5, which focuses on conflict management and peacebuilding. Different types of conflict demand distinctive approaches to peace, although recognizing the roles of ethnicity in all forms of regional civil war suggests a need to seriously consider ethnicity when promoting peace. At a broader level, communist and secessionist insurgencies are both declining. It is important to recognize that this decline is not automatic, with many grassroots and elite efforts helping to facilitate peace. Communist and secessionist conflicts meet different ends, with communist conflicts typically ending in some sort of insurgent defeat, whereas secessionist conflicts are amenable to compromise through territorial autonomy and have a continued threat of recurrence. Communal conflicts, however, are not declining, lacking the sort of arcs found in insurgencies. As a result, understanding how to resolve, or more accurately manage, tensions demands greater appreciation for grassroots and ethnically informed approaches to peace. Traditional leaders, shared customs, sacred symbols, and local ceremonies help to diminish violence in Southeast Asia but are especially relevant in mitigating the types of conflict that continue to threaten the peoples of the region.

2 Revolutionary Conflicts

Consider the following account: Peace talks between the government and the Communist Party of the Philippines (CPP) and its affiliates held promise, but the two sides could not compromise over land reform and income equality. When talks failed, the CPP reaffirmed its commitment to overthrowing the president through national revolution. The CPP launched attacks in several provinces, killing dozens. The Philippine president announced the formation of anti-communist militias and declared the communists to be enemies of the state. In a press release, government officials stated that war was necessary, as the CPP "do not really want peace, they want power" (Arcilla 2019). These events could have easily taken place in the 1960s, part of a Cold War communist insurgency supported by Maoist China or the Soviet Union. Instead, they occurred in 2019, decades after the Cold War ended.

This section provides an overview of revolutionary conflicts in Southeast Asia. A key theme is the importance of ethnic identity in shaping these conflicts. Even though they may seem to be based on material and ideological factors, with many communists denying the relevance of ethnicity, revolutionary conflicts feature important roles for ethnic identity. This is not to say that they are really about ethnicity instead of class but rather that ethnic dimensions are underappreciated and interact with class in interesting ways in such conflicts. This section illustrates some broad temporal patterns, with revolutionary conflicts mostly beginning in the 1950s and then declining in the late 1970s and the 1980s. After a brief conceptual discussion, this section discusses several Southeast Asian revolutionary insurgencies, organized in terms of conflict outcome (Mason, Weingarten & Fett 1999): successful revolutions, failed revolutions, and active conflicts.

2.1 Understanding Revolutions

All Southeast Asian countries have been marked by revolutionary violence. Together, Southeast Asian revolutionary conflicts have killed millions, injuring and traumatizing many more, and their scars remain visible today. Long after the Cold War, communist revolutions and insurgencies still matter. After all, two of ten Southeast Asian countries are ruled by communist parties (Vietnam and Laos), with a third led by former communist leaders (Cambodia). As Levitsky and Way (2013, 5) suggest, "revolutionary regimes are remarkably durable." Countries such as Malaysia and Indonesia remain scarred by communist and anti-communist violence, with ongoing debates over their legacies. And, as noted, at least one Southeast Asian country remains home to an active revolutionary insurgency.

Mid-twentieth-century Southeast Asia provided fertile soil for the rise of communist movements. Southeast Asian societies were largely agrarian, with wealth concentrated in small urban centers and states possessing limited reach in impoverished countrysides. For van der Kroef (1981, 147), the appeal of communism rose in tandem with the "spreading polarization of landholdings, along with the steady growth of the landless proletariat." Peasant societies suffered in the shadow of highly unequal access to land, promoting many Southeast Asian governments to attempt land reform to quell communist threats. Meanwhile, oppressive colonial orders crumbled, accelerated by Japanese invasions that left their own bitter legacies as well as military training and equipment. With communist revolution in China and continued Soviet expansion, Southeast Asian communist movements found inspiration as well as material support. The 1950s also saw regional economic stagnation, as the Pacific War and anti-colonial struggles led to moribund economies, widespread grievances, and a vacuum of authority.

Revolutionary conflicts have several distinctive features compared to other forms of violence. While ethnic conflicts are largely centrifugal, pushing out to the periphery, revolutionary conflicts tend to be centripetal, seeking to capture the center of power. Revolutionaries aim for the national government and capital city, even if many find refuge in remote countrysides (where they may encounter distinctive ethnic minorities). Revolutionaries present visions of an ideal society and a criticism of the status quo.[1] Revolutionary movements are typically highly organized, with parties, publications, armed divisions, and affiliate organizations for women, workers, and youth (Pye 1956). They also tend to be susceptible to doctrinal splits. In Southeast Asia, some communist movements embraced Maoist models, focusing on the peasantry and finding support from China, while others enjoyed Soviet assistance. These and other political/doctrinal divisions make for distinctive patterns of violence.

Communist revolutionaries are typically uninterested in ethnic differences, seeking unity among the exploited classes. Marx (1848) saw racial, ethnic, and nationalist divisions as promoted by capitalist classes to divide the poor, emphasizing that "the working men have no country." Communists initially spoke of transcending borders, races, and nations. Many saw ethnicity and minority nationalism as destined to melt away once class consciousness evolved. In Indonesia, communists featured an "ideological rejection of ethnic boundaries" that sometimes clashed with popular sensibilities (McVey 2006, 225). Despite this, revolutionary movements contain ethnic dimensions. All communist revolutions in Southeast Asia have featured at least some

---

[1] Some mention should be made of religious revolutionary conflicts. Despite obvious differences regarding faith, religious revolutionaries resemble communists, being organized through cadres with highly developed social networks, a firm sense of certainty, and a tendency to target rival interpretations. Southeast Asia has seen various religious radicals fighting to remake national politics and society. The clearest case of Islamic revolutionary conflict was Indonesia's Darul Islam Rebellion (DI). The DI originated in the 1940s around West Java, with regional Islamic strongholds in Sulawesi and Aceh joining the rebellion in the 1950s. In a sense, the DI was simultaneously central and periphery-seeking (Sjamsuddin 1985). It ended in 1962, having killed over 30,000 people.

ethno-nationalist themes, and most framed themselves as national liberation movements. Communist nationalism was sometimes obscured by a tendency to see revolutionary conflicts in terms of Cold War geopolitics. As McVey (2006, xiv) observes, any study of a communist movement "must decide whether to consider the party primarily as a component of a world movement or to view it as part of the domestic political scene." Echoing this, Weiss (2020, 511) suggests that Malaysia's communist conflict "fits better within a narrative of anti-colonialism and contestation over national identity and institutions than one of superpower rivalries." When we approach communist movements in terms of domestic politics, their ethnic dimensions become more visible.

Benedict Anderson (1991, 3) emphasizes how ethnicity and nationalism permeated communist movements. Anderson cites Hobsbawm regarding the nationalist character of all revolutionary movements, as well as Nairn's suggestion that nationalism "represents Marxism's great historical failure." Anderson's *Imagined Communities* begins with observations on wars between China, Vietnam, and Cambodia, in which communist governments placed realpolitik and rival nationalisms ahead of shared ideology. After all, communists tend to be organized by country, with international groupings such as the Indochinese Communist Party giving way to parties based on ethno-national identities.

Revolutionary insurgencies tend to be waged by specific ethnic groups, which find recruits and supporters in ethnic strongholds while failing to make inroads in other ethnic communities. Southeast Asian revolutionary movements were generally associated with particular ethnic communities, perhaps those that were less religious but especially those facing exclusion or exploitation. Communist insurgencies are especially likely to attract dedicated recruits when class inequality intersects with ethnic inequality. Intersections of class and ethnic inequalities – of ranked ethnic groups – tend to result in revolutionary messages appealing to some ethnic groups more than others. When this is not the case, and communists draw from multiple ethnic groups, there is then a danger of ethnic divisions within communist movements. Finally, some communist movements faced opposition from particular ethnic groups, often those motivated by religious beliefs or long-standing opposition to pro-communist ethnic majorities. Some of the most dedicated anti-communist resistance in Southeast Asia has been found among small minorities such as hill communities.

Just as communists tend to look down on ethnicity and nationalism, they also tend to look down on religion – as an opiate of the masses, in Marx's famous phrase. As a consequence, many revolutionary insurgencies criticized or sought to control religion, despite there being opportunities to find common ground with religious activists. Although there were also some instances of communists courting religious leaders, overall the tensions between communism and religion meant that some of the most passioned anti-revolutionary sentiment was found among religious groups. For example, communist persecution of religion in Vietnam led many Buddhist and Christian groups to flee to the south, causing South Vietnam to become identified with Catholicism while Buddhist groups led powerful social movements (Topmiller 2002).

Highlighting the neglected roles of ethnicity and religion in Southeast Asian revolutionary conflicts allows us to recognize some consistencies across Southeast Asian conflicts. Although communist insurgencies involve some distinct features, they also share some causes and grievances with secessionist and communal ethnic conflicts. Such similarities underline the importance of taking ethnicity into account for the sake of conflict management. Although such grievances are less likely to translate into communist violence today, if unaddressed they may manifest in other forms of violence.

2.2 Successful Revolutions

Three communist revolutions overthrew postcolonial governments and took power in Southeast Asia. The three countries – Vietnam, Cambodia, and Laos – are all contiguous parts of the former French Indochina. It is difficult to discuss the conflicts that gave rise to these governments purely as revolutionary civil wars, since they were intertwined with independence struggles and Cold War geopolitics and thus had elements of intrastate and interstate conflicts. It is also difficult to distinguish violence resulting from revolutionaries capturing power from the violence unleashed once they held it.

The Vietnam War began as an independence struggle in an age of communist resistance. As has been noted in Southeast Asia as a whole, the Cold War had a "walk-on part" in the drama of decolonization (Guan 2018, 9), with anti-colonial conflicts distorted by US and Soviet interests. Ho Chi Minh and his party were nationalist, anti-colonial forces, but communism then provided a dominant language of resistance and presented a compelling critique of colonialism.[2] The Communist Party of Vietnam (CPV) was formed in 1930 and featured nationalist themes, but it was soon renamed the Indochinese Communist Party (ICP) at the behest of the Comintern to include Laos and Cambodia. As St. John (2006, 6) observes, "Vietnamese revolutionaries toiled over the next decade with little success to recruit members in Cambodia and Laos." Similarly, Henley (1995, 316) suggests that the ICP was unsuccessful

---

[2] This said, Tuong Vu (2016) suggests that Vietnamese foreign policy was often driven by ideology more than patriotism, cautioning against overemphasizing nationalism in Vietnamese communism.

"in recruiting Khmer and Lao members" as it was largely an ethnic Vietnamese organization.

World War II presented unique challenges for Vietnamese communists and nationalists. With France occupied by Germany, the French colonial regime was weakened. Representing occupied France, colonial authorities were technically allied with Japan, "in an uneasy state of co-existence" (Christie 2001, 83). Whereas other Asian independence movements had to discern the lesser of two evils – European or Japanese colonizers – in Indochina they were one and the same, simplifying American decisions to support the Vietnamese resistance (the Vietminh) (Batholomew-Feis 2006). In 1945, Ho Chi Minh declared the independence of Vietnam, not Indochina, criticizing the French for using colonial borders to "destroy the national unity" of the Vietnamese (Ho 1945). The Vietminh were positioned to lead an independent Vietnam, but the Allies agreed that France would reoccupy Indochina, aided by Chinese nationalist troops in the north and British Indian troops in the south. The Vietminh resisted French efforts to reestablish colonial rule in the First Indochina War (1946–54). As the Cold War expanded, the United States began supporting France in Indochina. By 1954, the Vietminh controlled much of northern and central Vietnam, while France controlled southern regions, urban areas, and parts of Cambodia and Laos. The final battle was a famous communist victory at Dienbienphu. However, the 1954 Geneva Conference ended with the Americans taking over for France, leading into the Second Indochina War (1955–75).

In the north, the Communists led a social revolution, executing Japanese/ French collaborators, including many landlords. They also worked to rebuild infrastructure, expand literacy, and eradicate "social ills" (Luong 1992, 144). The 1953 land reform program saw thousands killed in the name of redistribution. Communist persecution led many minorities and religious groups to flee south. This was especially true of Catholic minorities, who were well-represented in South Vietnam, while Buddhists struggled under both the communists and the United States–allied Diem regime (Topmiller 2006). The United States supported Diem's brutal regime until his execution in 1963, an event which began a revolving door of military presidents in South Vietnam. In 1968, communists organized the Tet Offensive, striking key points in South Vietnam and helping to sway US public opinion. Ho Chi Minh died soon after, with USA–Vietnam peace talks ushering in a US withdrawal in 1973. Vietnam was unified under communist rule in 1975. While a communist revolution, the war was also a Vietnamese national liberation struggle, with the goal of independence likely prompting more sacrifice than did Marxism.

The Cambodian Revolution unfolded very differently. Despite claiming to represent the entire colony, the ICP was mostly ethnic Vietnamese. In 1951, it fragmented into ethnic Vietnamese, Cambodian, and Lao parties. Separated from Vietnamese domination, the Khmer People's Revolutionary Party grew quickly. In the late 1950s, Cambodian communists split into pro- and anti-Vietnam factions, with the latter becoming the Maoist Khmer Rouge. Communist uprisings expanded in 1968, beginning the Cambodian civil war. In 1970, a US-backed coup overthrew the government, with the new regime embarking on anti-Vietnamese pogroms that killed thousands and displaced half of the country's 450,000 ethnic Vietnamese (Ehrentraut 2011, 785). The military regime's primary enemy, the Khmer Rouge, also saw growing tensions with Vietnam. Chandler (1991, 2016) writes: "Many Cambodian Communists shared racially based ideas about Vietnam with their countrymen who had executed Vietnamese civilians in May 1970." The Khmer Rouge opted to align with China, moving away from Vietnamese and Soviet influence. The Khmer Rouge took control in 1975 and set the calendar to Year Zero.

Although the Khmer Rouge was communist, its violence involved ethnic Khmer nationalism and a deep xenophobia. Emptying the cities was intended to purge foreign influences and return to an agrarian Khmer golden age. The Khmer Rouge targeted ethnic minorities, religions, those familiar with foreign languages, and others. Kiernan (2002, 9) explains how Cambodians could be killed if they appeared in any way "contaminated by foreign influence." The Khmer Rouge conducted internal purges, attacking those with Vietnamese connections and forcing thousands of Cambodians to flee to Vietnam. In 1978, Vietnam and its Cambodian allies invaded Cambodia. Vietnamese forces captured much of the country, with the Khmer Rouge mounting guerrilla resistance. Tellingly, the Khmer Rouge then renounced communism in place of Cambodian nationalism, gaining assistance from China and the United States to fight against the Vietnamese occupation. Vietnam withdrew from Cambodia in 1991, with the transition led by the United Nations (UN) leading to an independent Cambodia in 1993. Hun Sen, a former pro-Vietnam Khmer Rouge leader, emerged as prime minister, establishing an authoritarian regime that has endured for decades.

While they were international and revolutionary civil wars, the Vietnamese and Cambodian conflicts contained important ethnic subcurrents. Anderson (1991, 2) observes that "every successful revolution has defined itself in national terms." Vietnamese communists were nationalists, fighting an independence war against Western colonizers to unify their country. For some, the VCP's "true" nationalism is key to understanding its victory over the South, which was promoting a "fake nationalism" alongside foreign occupiers (Race 1973, 182). For Luong (1992, 168), although the Vietnamese revolution contained other elements, national liberation represented "the primary objective for the majority of Vietnamese." Kalyvas and Kocher (2007, 197) demonstrate that "the Vietnam War had a significant ethnic dimension," with ethnic and religious minorities supporting the government against the communists. As China and Vietnam went to war in 1979, Vietnam experienced violence against ethnic Chinese residents, resulting in hundreds dying and tens of thousands displaced (Chang 1982). Meanwhile, the ethnic overtones of the Khmer Rouge were readily apparent, as their peasant nationalism and xenophobia sometimes outweighed their Marxism – "Khmer Rouge conceptions of race overshadowed those of class" (Kiernan 2002, 26). Anti-Vietnamese sentiment was shared by the Lon Nol regime and Khmer Rouge. Today, Hun Sen, once pro-Vietnam and anti-China, has returned to traditional patterns, allying with China and clashing with Vietnam.

The third communist revolution unfolded in Laos. Early on, Lao communism was dominated by "Vietnamese émigrés," as the ICP featured few Lao recruits (Goscha 2003, 279). The Pathet Lao emerged from the ICP in 1955 but retained Vietnamese influence. Laos experienced clashes between US-backed royalists and Vietnamese-backed communists, with tens of thousands dying in a civil war. After 1968, the United States began arming and training the country's ethnic minorities, notably the Hmong in the mountainous highlands (Hamilton-Merritt 1993). The Pathet Lao took power in 1975. Lao communists were not as intent on purging religion or eliminating markets, although opposition parties and free media were eliminated. Communist Laos has remained dependent on Vietnam, although even here there have been tensions. A 1983 Vietnamese statement proclaiming a goal to rebuild "Indochina" was met with Khmer and Lao resistance, with Hanoi seeing solidarity undermined by "age-old ethnic prejudices" (Pouvatchy 1986, 450). The US-backed Hmong insurgency continued, with sporadic violence even decades after the Cold War. Again, there are important ethnic dimensions, with Lao communists fighting various hill tribes.

Southeast Asia's three communist revolutions all took place in neighboring mainland Southeast Asian countries that comprised the former French colony of Indochina. These successful communist revolutions can be explained by several factors, but their fusion with nationalism was especially important, as powerful communist parties embodied anti-colonial nationalism.

2.3 Failed Communist Insurgencies

The aforementioned revolutions featured ethno-nationalist dimensions intertwined with ideology. Communist forces were popular nationalists and faced resistance from ethnic minorities. Similar dynamics were found in Southeast Asia's failed communist insurgencies and movements, although in these cases sitting governments held nationalist credentials, often framing communists as foreign. Here I discuss communist insurgencies in Myanmar, Malaysia, Thailand, and Indonesia, conflicts defeated by their host states at great cost.

Communism grew in what was then known as Burma in the 1930s, with early influences coming from India. In 1939, the Indian Communist Party created a party in Burma. The party elected Aung San as its leader, but in reality, much of the Communist Party of Burma (CPB) was Bengali (Taylor 1983, 99). This put the CPB in a difficult position, as it needed Indian support and promoted internationalism but also needed nationalist credentials in a largely anti-Indian Burmese society. World War II presented a challenge to the CPB, as ethnic Chinese and Indian members opposed Japanese fascism, while ethnic Burmese admired Japan and welcomed independence. In 1946, the CPB saw its first major split, with the larger "white flags" working with the government to ensure independence while the more radical "red flags" took up arms against Britain and the Burmese government. The white flags enjoyed close connections to Aung San, especially CPB leader Than Tun, who was Aung San's brother-in-law. After the assassination of Aung San, the white flags also rebelled as Burma gained independence in 1948.

The CPB established zones of control in the center of the country, mobilizing a sizable People's Army. Its leadership was ethnic Burmese, Indian, and Chinese, with recruits drawn largely from disaffected minority communities, whose loyalty sometimes tended toward their ethnic communities. For example, the CPB expanded in Rakhine State until local leftists broke away in 1962 to form an ethnic Rakhine communist party. The communist insurgency slowed in the late 1950s as the government offered amnesties and pivoted left. Under General Ne Win after 1962, the Burmese government proclaimed itself socialist, taking over the economy, promoting "Burmanization," and severing international ties. The shift toward isolationism was both socialist and ethno-nationalist, as the government pushed out ethnic Indian and Chinese minorities while nationalizing larger businesses. Nevertheless, the Ne Win regime was hardly pro-communist. In the 1960s, the CPB experienced internal purges influenced by China's Cultural Revolution (Holmes 1967). The red flags were defeated in 1978, but the CPB continued its fight. After the 1988 student-led uprising, the overthrow of Ne Win, and the end of the Cold War, the CPB was at a crossroads. In 1989, a dramatic internal mutiny saw communist soldiers turn on their leaders, who fled to China. The end of the conflict "reflected ethnic tensions within the party," as "the overwhelming majority of the CPB rank-and-file comes from various minority forces . . . motivated by ethnicity and general anti-government sentiments rather than ideology" (Lintner 1990, 1). The downfall of the CPB reflected tensions inherent since its inception, with minorities ending the insurgency and forming an ethnic army.

Malaysia also saw a sizable communist movement, again with prominent ethnic divisions. The Malayan Communist Party (MCP) was created in 1930 as the successor to China's South Seas Communist Party. Operating across modern Malaysia and Singapore, its support was found mostly among Chinese trade unions. The MCP grew in its struggle against the Japanese Occupation, in which the occupiers targeted ethnic Chinese. As the British returned, the MCP organized strikes and attacked British targets, leading to the 1948 "Emergency." The British fought communist insurgents with tactics later mirrored by the Americans in Vietnam, creating "New Villages" to deprive communists of civilian support. The Emergency officially ended in 1960, although fighting continued near the Thai border through 1989. Malaysia's communist insurgency featured clear ethnic dimensions. The MCP was rooted in ethnic Chinese communities, especially Chinese schools and trade unions. The MCP has been described as "a predominantly ethnic Chinese revolutionary organization" (Nathan 1990, 210) and "essentially a Chinese affair: a Chinese communist party, Chinese guerrillas, Chinese support – and Chinese victims" (Short 1970, 1081). For Guan (2018, 19), the MCP's primary weakness "was its inability to recruit Malays and Indians." This is not to suggest that the MCPs was entirely Chinese; it found some support among Malays influenced by Indonesian activism and featured a largely ethnic Malay 10th Regiment (Weiss 2020). Overall, however, Malaysia's communist insurgency was shaped a great deal by ethnic identity.

Thailand's experience with communism was shaped by its proximity to Vietnam, Cambodia, and Laos. According to the so-called domino theory, Thailand was at risk of falling as communist revolutions emanated outward from Indochina. Communism arrived in Thailand in the 1920s, largely through Chinese migrants, but the Communist Party of Thailand (CPT) did not form until 1942 (Guan 2018, 24). Stuart-Fox (1979, 334) suggests that, by the 1950s, four communist parties were active in Thailand: "the Malay Communist Party in the far south, the ICP in the northeast, the Chinese Communist Party of Thailand (CCPT) among overseas Chinese, and the CPT." The CPT was mostly an ethnic Thai organization, but it was guided by the CCPT until their 1949 merger. The CPT launched an insurgency in 1965, primarily from its stronghold in the country's northeast region of Isan. Isan was and remains one of the country's poorest regions, and it maintains a regional Lao ethnic identity. The CPT thus featured pro-Beijing Sino-Thai leadership and ethnic Lao recruits influenced by the Soviets through Laos. The 1970s saw political instability and, after government attacks on students, expanded CPT recruitment. The insurgency waned in the 1980s, with the government offering amnesties to student recruits. Divisions among Thai communists, Thailand's rapid economic growth, and the end of the Cold War helped to end the insurgency by the 1990s. Ethnic divisions contributed significantly to the CPT's downfall. The most important chasm was between the CPT's base in Isan – which promoted "pan-Laoism" and partnership with pro-Soviet Indochinese communists – and the pro-China leadership (Stuart-Fox 1979, 351). The conflict also had ethnic dimensions in the north, where recruits were from disadvantaged hill tribes, and in the south, where many Malay recruits later joined secessionist movements.

The final major defeated communist movement is the Partai Komunis Indonesia (PKI). At one time, the PKI appeared poised to take power through its participation in government and, potentially, carry out a social revolution. With some 2–3 million members and the ear of President Sukarno, Indonesian communists held considerable sway. But in 1965–6, the PKI was eradicated in a spate of horrific violence. As a result, the PKI never mounted the sort of mass insurgency found in other countries. This said, its size, brief revolutionary uprisings, and violent end make it important to discuss in terms of revolutionary conflicts.

What became the PKI was formed in 1914. Although beset by factionalism, the PKI was highly organized, featuring a slew of affiliate labor, peasant, women's, and youth organizations. Many PKI leaders, especially early on, saw Islam and communism as compatible, making inroads with Islamic organizations through shared commitments to egalitarianism, justice, and nationalism. After being banned by colonial authorities, the PKI reemerged in the war for independence. The PKI was involved in the disastrous 1948 Madiun Affair, in which communists in Central Java fought Indonesian Republican forces. This failed uprising had important legacies, as the communists were seen as betraying the national independence movement. After Madiun, the PKI attached itself to President Sukarno and the nationalist cause. The PKI was officially pan-ethnic but found support in specific groups; unlike insurgent communist groups elsewhere, it was strongest at the center rather than the periphery. For Lev (1967, 27), the PKI's vision was "beyond both ethnic and traditional socio-religious distinctions . . . even though it was a predominantly Javanese party." In the 1955 elections, the PKI received most of its votes in Central and East Java, with limited support in the pious Sundanese West Java. Only 10 percent of PKI votes came from outside of Java, mostly in Javanese plantation zones in Sumatra.

As President Sukarno amassed power, he aligned with the PKI as a means to offset the army. This process came to a head in 1965. At the time, rumors were rampant that either the army or the PKI would lead a coup. A group of leftist military officers proceeded to murder several generals and call for a new government. Over the next year, the army, gangsters, and religious groups led in the slaughter of accused communists, killing over half a million people (Robinson 2018). The PKI and the killings of 1965–6 again had ethnic dimensions. The PKI drew disproportionately from ethnic Javanese, especially *abangan*, or syncretic Muslims (Ricklefs 2012). Meanwhile, religious groups and military strongholds tended to be found in the Outer Islands. The ethnic dimensions should not be exaggerated, however – Robinson (2018, 132) reminds us that, in 1965, "Javanese Muslims killed Javanese Muslims, Balinese Hindus killed Balinese Hindus, Protestant Bataks killed Protestant Bataks, Florenese Catholics killed Florenese Catholics, and so on."

These failed communist movements feature important differences compared to the successful revolutions. While in Vietnam and Cambodia communists represented the ethnic majorities and were seen as nationalist movements, this was less the case in Myanmar, Malaysia, and Thailand, where communists were framed by authorities as foreign and dominated by minorities. In other words, communist success in large part depended on their nationalist credentials in relation to their governments. In the failed cases, communist forces featured internal ethnic divisions, and some were associated with minority groups and with foreign powers, notably China; in Indonesia the party was rooted in the country's largest ethnic group (the Javanese) but faced a formidable communal rival in the shape of the country's pious Islamic community. In all four cases, the incumbent state maintained some nationalist credentials and a degree of capacity, enabling government supporters to successfully portray the communists as foreign.

2.4 Ongoing Communist Insurgencies

Southeast Asia's last major ongoing revolutionary insurgency is found in the Philippines, where the CPP, the New People's Army (NPA), and affiliated groups have waged guerrilla conflict for over half a century. The CPP was created in 1968, but its origins go back to the 1930s, when American colonial authorities outlawed communist organizations (Guan 2018, 22). Another antecedent of the NPA was the Hukbalahap ("Huk") movement of the 1940s. Originating in central Luzon against Japanese occupation forces, the Huks rebelled against landowners and the government after the Japanese were expelled. The conflict declined in the early 1950s through amnesties and land grants to settle Mindanao (McKenna 1998, 115). Kerkvliet (1977, 99) suggests that, despite some coordination, the Huks were not formally affiliated with the CPP but were a product of agrarian social conditions.

The Philippines has perpetual problems of growing populations, rural inequality, and powerful oligarchic, landowning families, together creating fertile grounds for communist movements. The Maoist CPP/NPA launched an insurgency in 1969 across the Philippines, breaking away from the aging pro-Soviet leadership in the Partido Komunista ng Pilipinas (PKP). This revival prompted President Marcos to declare martial law in 1972, a move also intended to extend his rule and eliminate his rivals. The CPP continued its insurgency, mostly in Luzon and northern Mindanao, through the 1980s. The "People Power" overthrow of Marcos in 1986 put the CPP in a difficult position, as it applauded the president's removal but did not play a leading role in the movement, and democratization left Philippine social hierarchy intact. For Sison (2004, 114), "it was not possible for the communists openly to take a share of power in the coalition government [because] the ruling system and its armed forces were intact." In 1994, President Ramos legalized the communist party and offered amnesties, but the insurgency continued.

There are several reasons why the Philippines stands out as home to the only significant remaining communist insurgency in Southeast Asia – and one of the few such surviving in the world. One factor is continuing inequality and landlessness, exacerbated by a growing population and poor economic planning. To sustain their movement, the CPP has cultivated broad networks of support. The CPP "maintains an overlapping and intersecting series of organizations that constitute the 'popular front,'" including groups such as the National Democratic Front, a Christian-affiliated liberation theology group, as well as organizations focusing on women, youth, and farmers (Magno & Gregor 1986, 503). The CPP maintains diverse operations across the country, sometimes linked to prominent politicians and criminal networks. Another factor sustaining the insurgency is that it has not been beset by deep ethnic divisions. The CPP established strongholds among many minority groups, especially hill communities, whose mountainous homes suit guerrilla warfare (Paredes 1997). It is estimated that the majority of NPA recruits in Mindanao are members of indigenous communities (Simbulan 2016). Although the CPP is popular in Mindanao, it has not made inroads into Muslim communities, where secessionist movements have dominated (see Section 3). The conflict thus has ethnic elements, but fewer than other Southeast Asian communist movements. This partly explains the exceptional durability of revolutionary conflict in the Philippines, as the CPP has not attached itself to a particular ethnic group or met determined opposition from rival ethnic groups.

2.5 Conclusions

Communist movements have featured in every Southeast Asian country, including those not mentioned such as Singapore and Brunei. The human toll of the region's communist conflicts has been significant. Table 1 summarizes the revolutionary conflicts discussed in this section, providing estimates from the PRIO database and secondary sources. Although it is difficult to estimate casualties for any particular conflict, especially those with extensive foreign involvement, it is clear that Southeast Asia's revolutionary conflicts have been immensely destructive.

Based on these estimates, Figure 2 visualizes broad trends in revolutionary conflicts. Estimates are taken from the PRIO fatality dataset, adding the casualties from the revolutionary conflicts listed, then coded as five-year averages. I have tried to exclude casualties associated with direct American involvement as well as violence perpetrated by the Khmer Rouge regime (between Cambodian civil wars), although the figure includes anti-communist violence in Indonesia. Figure 2 shows that revolutionary conflicts killed millions, representing the leading form of violence in the region, but also reveals a sharp decline from the late 1970s. As new regimes were consolidated by the 1980s, be they revolutionary or counterrevolutionary, governments were able to suppress revolutionary sentiment through development, amnesties, military assaults, or some combination of the three. By the 1990s, communist insurgencies were nearly eliminated; except for in the Philippines, revolutionary insurgencies appear to be consigned to the past.

In discussing revolutions that succeeded in capturing power alongside those that failed or remain active, this section emphasized important yet underappreciated ethnic dimensions in communist insurgencies. Although communists typically reject ethnic and national divisions, most communists drew strength from particular ethnic groups and featured nationalist messages. Communist parties have been undermined by internal ethnic divisions, and many have faced opposition from specific ethno-religious groups. This is not to suggest that they are, at their core, ethnic conflicts. Class and ideology were obviously critical in each of these insurgencies, and, as we will see in the sections to come, class inequalities are also critical factors in ethnic conflicts. Instead, approaching revolutionary conflicts from an ethnic perspective helps us to understand them in new ways and draws key similarities with other forms of lethal conflict. Ethnic factors also help to explain the relative strength of various communist insurgencies: movements that have successfully portrayed themselves as nationalists were able to succeed, while those that could be framed as alien and featured ethnic schisms were less likely to do so.

Table 1 Major revolutionary conflicts in Southeast Asia

Country	Insurgents	Duration	Outcome	Casualties
Philippines	Huks	1942–54	Defeated	≈10,000[1]
Vietnam	CPV, Vietminh	1945–75	Revolution	Unclear, overlap with anti-colonial /interstate[2]
Malaysia	MCP	1948–89	Defeat	≈11,000[3]
Burma	CPB (white flags) CP (red flags)	1948–89	Defeat	≈17,000–170,000[4]
Indonesia	Darul Islamic	1949–62	Defeat	≈10,000–20,000[5]
Cambodia	Khmer Rouge	1951–80	Revolution	Unclear, overlap with other conflicts[6]
Laos	Pathet Lao	1955–75	Revolution	≈20,000[7]
Thailand	CPT	1964–90s	Defeat	≈5,000–9,000[8]
Indonesia	PKI	1965–6	Defeat	≈500,000[9]
Philippines	CPP / NPA	1969–	Ongoing	≈40,000[10]

1. PRIO estimates 10,000 casualties, providing a range of 9,000–19,000 (1946–54).
2. PRIO estimates 370,000 casualties in the independence war with France (1946–54), 165,000 in the interwar period (1955–64), and 1,460,000 in the United States–Vietnam War (1965–75). COW (Sarkees & Wayman 2010) estimates 100,000 casualties in intrastate violence (1961–5).
3. PRIO estimates 11,400 casualties, providing a range of 7,963–12,882 (1948–57) and 138–3,213 after 1957. COW codes this an anti-colonial war, estimating 9,100 casualties (1948–57).
4. PRIO estimates 17,600–170,375 casualties (1949–89). COW combines communist and Karenni secessionist conflicts, estimating 40,000 casualties.
5. PRIO codes Darul Islam in 1953, then combines it with the Permesta Rebellion for 1958–61, estimated 1,000–35,000 casualties. COW estimates 3,000 casualties in 1953.
6. PRIO estimates several thousand casualties in the independence war with France (1946–53) and about 500,000 in intrastate conflicts (1965–98).
7. PRIO estimates several thousand casualties in the independence war with France (1946–53) and about 20,000 in intrastate conflicts (1959–90). COW estimates approximately 25,000 casualties.
8. PRIO estimates 3,350 casualties (1974–82). COW estimates 2200 casualties in 1972–73.
9. From Robinson (2018). Neither PRIO nor COW feature estimates because this was not an armed conflict.
10. PRIO estimates 21,000–46,000 casualties (1969–2008). COW estimates 31,000 casualties (1972–92).

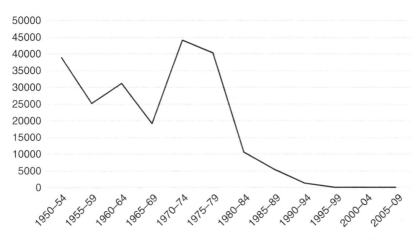

Figure 2 Casualty estimates, Southeast Asian revolutionary conflicts

Source: PRIO 2012, coded as five-year averages

3 Secessionist Conflicts

In January 2019, thousands of ethnic Karen people and various armed organizations came together in eastern Myanmar to commemorate a conflicted occasion: the seventieth anniversary of the Karen independence movement. The Karen conflict is perhaps the world's longest-running civil war and may be one of the most complex. Karen communities feature numerous divisions and fluid edges, with various armed groups and political loyalties. The "Revolution Day" celebration featured parades, folk dances, traditional theatre, and several speeches. It brought together various rebel groups but also former rebels now integrated into Burmese security forces to fight against them. Through numerous factions, co-optations, and ceasefires, thousands have been killed and hundreds of thousands endure cycles of displacement. Seventy years on, a tentative ceasefire paused the conflict, with the anniversary celebration punctuated by occasional mortar fire (Sanford 2019).

This section analyzes secessionist insurgencies in Southeast Asia. After discussing their logic and the roles of ethnicity, it presents case overviews, again organized by conflict outcomes. There are two important differences from Section 2, however. For one, it is hard to speak of failed secessionist movements and clear-cut state victories. Unlike communist insurgencies, secessionist conflicts tend to feature periods of dormancy, only to reemerge years later. A secessionist organization may be defeated, but larger secessionist struggles tend to recur. This cyclical pattern echoes findings in the civil war literature – that post–Cold War insurgencies tend to fizzle, declining in intensity instead of resulting in a clear outcome (Lyall & Wilson 2009). Second, unlike communist insurgencies, secessionist conflicts are sometimes resolved through another potential outcome – compromise through territorial autonomy. This section also observes broad trends over time. Like revolutionary insurgencies, secessionist insurgencies see a clear arc and then decline, although this arc unfolds two decades later than the communist arc and the decline is not as dramatic. We thus see ways in which revolutionary and secessionist conflicts feature underappreciated similarities but also important differences.

3.1 Secessionism

Secessionism represents a political campaign by territorially concentrated minorities to attain formal statehood. Separatism is a related, wider term that refers to efforts to increase self-government and distance from the host state (Wood 1981). The distinction is important, as secessionist demands may shift to separatism if rebels see genuine opportunities for self-government. Separatism may be violent or nonviolent, depending especially on the host state; however, secessionism is typically violent (Brancati 2006, 654).[3]

Although authors typically analyze them separately or emphasize their differences, secessionist conflicts resemble revolutionary conflicts in many ways. Both are rebel insurgencies, with armed groups fighting state forces to bring political change for marginalized groups. Indeed, communist movements inspired many secessionist leaders, who saw their groups as exploited by host states. Revolutionary and secessionist insurgencies feature armed groups that seek to control territory, with the most intense violence found in areas contested between state and rebel forces (Kalyvas 2006). Rebel strongholds see armed groups establishing local systems of order, often resulting in state-like forms of rebel governance (Arjona, Kasfir & Mampilly 2015).

Just as revolutionary conflicts feature important ethnic dimensions, secessionist conflicts intersect with class dimensions. Revolutionary movements typically seek to unite lower classes across ethnic groups, while secessionist movements typically seek to unite ethnic groups across classes. Secessionist leaders thus suppress class divisions within a given ethnic community, seeing ethnic elites as defending their group and the host state and national majority as the oppressors. Almost all secessionist regions feature grievances related to underdevelopment and exploitation at the hands of host states. However, secessionists typically see exploitation in terms of group rights, depicting national

---

[3] A related concept is irredentism, in which a territorially concentrated minority seeks to leave its host state and join another, co-ethnic state. Irredentism is somewhat rare, as elites stand to gain less from joining another state compared to ruling their own. As a result, irredentism tends to be a project of neighbouring states rather than a goal of minority groups.

governments and firms as violating the moral economies of minority communities (McCarthy 2007).

Despite similarities, the two forms of conflict also differ in important ways. Revolutionary conflicts are centripetal, focused on the center of power in a given country, while secessionism is centrifugal, pulling outward from the periphery. For Mampilly (2012, 74–5), "there are two basic objectives that a rebel organization can espouse: overthrowing the central government or carving out a discrete territory from the state shell that corresponds with the aspirations of the target population." The different types of insurgencies feature distinctive policies in their strongholds, with revolutionaries seeking to displace landlords and redistribute wealth, often focusing on the participation of women and the poor, while secessionists are more likely to develop ethnic identity and local nationalism, often elevating local elites and targeting local minorities. While revolutionary conflicts largely formed during the 1950s, in the independence era and early Cold War, secessionist conflicts in Southeast Asia developed in two waves: in response to the end of colonialism in the 1950s; and in response to centralizing postcolonial governments in the 1970s. No sizable new secessionist movements emerged after the 1980s. And while revolutionary movements often gained support from communist countries, secessionists found support from enemies of their host state or co-ethnics in other states. The emergence of secessionism is shaped by domestic factors, but its success "is determined largely by international politics" (Horowitz 1985, 230). As a result, powerful secessionist movements typically depict themselves as a state and appeal to the international community.

Secessionists typically offer various justifications for independence: they say their territory was illegally incorporated into the host state; they claim to represent a distinctive ethnic nation deserving self-determination; and they cite abuse by host states. The illegal incorporation argument focuses on history, stating that invasion or colonialism forced them to join the country. Almost all Southeast Asian secessionists make this argument in some form, especially East Timor and Papua. A second logic is the often-cited "Right of Self-Determination," one of Wilson's Fourteen Points later promoted by the UN. Intended to limit military interventions and dismantle European colonialism, this has been understood by secessionists to mean that every distinctive people deserves their own state. A third major logic involves an aggrieved minority citing exclusion, exploitation, physical abuses, or other indignities, with such abuses necessitating separation. State militaries tend to take heavy-handed responses to secessionism, committing human rights abuses to preserve national borders and thus generating support for secessionism as they combat it.

For human rights abuses, inequality, resource extraction, and symbolic injustices to be perceived in group terms and fuel secessionism, a community must possess a strong sense of ethnic identity. As Horowitz (1985, 230) observes, secessionism "is a special species of ethnic conflict" along with communal violence. Secessionists see their communities not just as ethnic groups but as nations deserving their own state. An important difference between an ethnic group and a nation is a sense of political self-rule. Almost by definition, ethnic groups fighting to achieve statehood see themselves as a nation. To assert their distinctiveness, secessionists typically pursue nation-building, authoring history texts, celebrating historical Golden Ages, elevating ethno-national symbols such as flags, and so on. For Smith (1979, 22), "political separatisms on behalf of ethnic groups presuppose an 'ethnic revival,' a growth of ethnic self-consciousness and solidarity." Secessionists typically seek to exaggerate differences between their group and the host states to make them appear incompatible. This often involves violence against minorities, those outside of the aspiring nation who threaten its distinctiveness (Barter 2015a).

3.2 Successful Independence

Despite the existence of numerous secessionist movements around the world, successful independence is rare. While sometimes championing the right of all "peoples" to self-determination, the world system is conservative, supporting the territorial integrity of host states (Fearon 2004). Moreover, the few cases of successful independence, such as South Sudan, Kosovo, Bangladesh, and Eritrea, have struggled, beset by poverty, legacies of war, and divisions that were muted during independence wars.

Southeast Asia is home to one successful secessionist movement. The circumstances under which East Timor achieved independence were indeed unique, involving a weakened Indonesian state and considerable international support. Crucially, East Timor was a Portuguese colony, unlike the rest of Indonesia, which was a former Dutch colony, so its incorporation into Indonesia was never fully accepted internationally, and its eventual independence represented a reversion to colonial borders. After early expansion into Southeast Asia, the Portuguese remained only in the remote half-island of East Timor. Portugal's 1974 Carnation Revolution thrust independence upon its colonies. In East Timor, a power struggle ensued between leftist and pro-Portuguese conservative independence leaders. The leftist Fretilin emerged as the stronger party, threatening Indonesia as well as the United States and Australia, which did not want a "Cuba" in the midst of maritime Southeast Asia. With Western blessings, Indonesia invaded, formally annexing East Timor in 1976 despite Portuguese and UN protests.

Fretilin immediately mobilized resistance, to which Indonesian forces responded with brutal violence. Although Fretilin was in some ways a Marxist revolutionary movement, it came to stress ethno-nationalism over time. The decline of communist rhetoric can be explained by external factors, with East Timorese activists seeking Western support, as well as internal factors, with East Timorese nationalism amplified by the Indonesian occupation (Anderson 1993). Fretilin leaders composed several nationalist texts. For example, Xanana Gusmão wrote "A History that Beats in the Maubere Soul" to stimulate East Timorese nationalism and sacrifice. Gusmão argued that the nation of East Timor predated Portuguese colonialism, thus projecting a timeless nationalism (Kammen 2003, 72). In the 1980s, Indonesian authorities banned the use of Portuguese in government and religious services in the territory, inadvertently encouraging the indigenous language Tetum to become the language of Timorese nationalism (Carey 1999, 85–6).

The 1991 Dili Massacre, in which Indonesian troops killed independence activists attending a funeral, brought Western attention just as the Cold War was giving way to concern for human rights. In 1996, East Timorese leaders were awarded the Nobel Peace Prize, further elevating Timor's visibility. Diplomatic pressure gained new importance after the 1997 Asian Financial Crisis and the 1998 fall of Indonesia's President Suharto. Desperate to distance himself from Suharto and needing Western support, new Indonesian president Habibie announced a referendum for East Timor. Overseen by a small UN presence, the August 1999 referendum saw over 78 percent vote for independence. In response, Indonesian security forces and allied Timorese militias unleashed a scorched-earth campaign, killing thousands and decimating the new country (Robinson 2009). Violence was halted by an Australia-led UN intervention, which supervised the transition toward independence in May 2002.

East Timor's independence was not won militarily but was instead a product of influential Timorese civilian activists, an international solidarity campaign, and Indonesian regime change. An estimated 100,000 people died under the Indonesian occupation (CAVR 2005). Although the country has faced many challenges, including coup attempts and riots, East Timor stands as a rare successful secessionist movement.

3.3 Unresolved Secessionism

Although successful independence is rare, definitive state victories are also uncommon in secessionist conflicts. Once widespread, secessionist sentiment is rarely defeated by force. More than revolutionary conflicts, secessionist struggles have a way of recurring, and it is difficult to say that a given secessionist struggle is ever finished. Several conflicts in Southeast Asia have declined to the extent that violence has diminished or the secessionist goals of violent groups become unclear, sometimes a result of migration or other demographic changes in the separatist region. Even in such cases, one cannot suggest with certainty that the desire for statehood has been entirely extinguished. This is explained by the centrality of ethnic identity in such conflicts, as grievances related to abuse and exclusion can surface years later in ways that are less common in class-based conflicts.

One of the few cases in which we might reasonably suggest that secessionism was defeated was the short-lived Republic of South Maluku (RMS) movement in Ambon, Indonesia. Historically, the Christian Ambonese were associated with Dutch colonialism, working as soldiers and bureaucrats. The Indonesian independence struggle was a brutal affair, sowing tensions between pro- and anti-Dutch communities. As Indonesian authorities centralized power, Ambonese leaders proclaimed independence in 1950. Indonesia defeated Ambonese secessionists within several months, with some resistance continuing in nearby islands. Since the 1950s, secessionism has rarely surfaced as a salient political threat in Ambon, despite some murmurings in the late 1990s and 2000s amid communal conflict, discussed in Section 4.

Papuan secessionism has proven more enduring. Like Maluku, the Papua conflict is rooted in Dutch colonialism. It is likely that Papua's fragmented geography, as an island dotted with massive mountains and valleys, has helped thwart Indonesian state control and the defeat of secessionism, especially compared to Ambon. However, these same geographical barriers also produced a fragmented secessionist movement. Historically, Papua was a colonial periphery until the twilight of Dutch rule. With Indonesian independence in 1949, the Dutch retained Papua to maintain a colonial empire and undermine the Indonesian Republic. The Dutch finally invested in Papua, expanding education, encouraging Christianity, creating local governments, and incubating Papuan nationalism (Penders 2002, 388–92). Diplomatic pressure forced the Dutch to abandon the territory, with the UN transferring power to Indonesia in 1963. In 1969, Indonesian authorities organized a highly questionable referendum, the Act of Free Choice, to cement their control over Papua. Indonesia rightly claims that the Dutch encouraged Papuan secessionism in the embers of colonial empire, but it is also evident that most Papuans did not and do not support Indonesian rule.

As Indonesia incorporated Papua into its territory, Papuan resistance began immediately with the mobilization of the Free Papua Movement and other armed groups. Secessionists worked to forge a sense of Papuan nationalism, emphasizing distinctive ethnic traditions, championing the Morning Star Flag, and more. A major element has been race, with secessionists emphasizing physical differences between Asian Indonesians and Melanesian Papuans, a sentiment amplified by Indonesian prejudice. For Viartasiwi (2018, 149), "the notion of racial difference as a reason to secede" has been a growing element of Papuan secessionism alongside a sense of Melanesian cultural distinctiveness and Christian networks across Oceania. Secessionists have also struggled with factionalism. Papua has a history of clan feuding, a form of communal violence, as well as strong coast/interior inequalities and religious divides. This fragmentation has undermined Papuan secessionism but may also make secessionism difficult to overcome, as there is no single group to negotiate with or defeat. In 2001, Indonesia granted Papua autonomy, an offer immediately undermined when the government carved off the province of West Papua. Despite several challenges, Papuan secessionism remains active, with sporadic attacks, public protests, and rebel statements keeping hope for independence alive. In 2019, Papua was rocked by a series of large protests following racist attacks on Papuan students in Java, with crowds openly defying Indonesian authorities and raising the Morning Star flag. The Papuan secessionist conflict has no end in sight, with Indonesia's current approach widely seen as having failed.

Although not subjected to formal colonial rule, Thailand has also seen secessionism at its periphery. The three southern Thailand provinces of Narathiwat, Pattani, and Yala, as well as parts of Songkhla, comprised the historical Sultanate of Patani, which was subjugated by Siam/Thailand in the nineteenth century. The 1960s saw the mobilization of various secessionist organizations such as PULO (Patani United Liberation Organization) and the BRN (National Revolutionary Front). Secessionists were divided over their goals, namely independence or Malaysian irredentism, as well as symbols, with some favoring royal traditions or Islamic or Western models. They were united, however, as ethnic Malays and Muslims (Harish 2006). After a decade of secessionist violence, the CPT's defeat and the government's cooperation with Malaysia allowed Thailand to focus on secessionism. Thai authorities borrowed from successful anti-communist policies, providing amnesties and development opportunities. By the mid-1990s, it seemed that secessionism had been defeated. However, violence returned to Patani in 2004, with a raid on a police outpost and several anonymous attacks. This new wave of violence is widely seen as a response to Prime Minister Thaksin's dismantling of regional institutions in order to expand his power (McCargo 2008, 7). This iteration of violence differs from earlier secessionism, as contemporary militants have not always made clear secessionist demands or taken credit for attacks, and much of their violence has targeted civilians and other soft targets, claiming some 7,000 lives as well as injuring 10,000 and displacing many more (DSW 2019). Thai authorities have struggled to understand or contain this new form of secessionist resistance.

Finally, Myanmar features a staggering array of secessionist movements. Like Papua, geography serves to limit state control of peripheral regions, thus sustaining secessionist conflict, but also limits rebel cohesion. As James Scott (2009, 178) observes, Myanmar's northern hills feature "a scattered, mobile pattern of residence and a fluid, acephalous social structure capable of easy fissioning and recombination." Colonial rule amplified fragmentation in northern Myanmar, with Britain creating separate ethnic states and encouraging missionary activity. As Burma prepared for independence, Aung San signed the 1947 Panglong Agreement with representatives from Shan, Kachin, and Chin communities, who joined Burma on the condition that they retain "full autonomy." Mon and Rakhine groups were not invited, as Burmese leaders considered them part of the country's core, and Karen leaders refused to participate. The Agreement informed Chapter Ten of the 1947 Constitution, which specifies that "every State shall have the right to secede from the Union ... within ten years from the date on which this Constitution comes into operation." This meant that, in theory, minority states would be able to leave the country if the Union was not to their liking. Immediately after Burmese independence, various communist and secessionist insurgencies erupted, including various secessionist struggles.

It is difficult to discuss armed secessionism in Myanmar succinctly, as the country presents myriad factions, names, side-switching, fragmentation, and mergers. Smaller armed groups are found among the country's six Self-Administered Zones, most of which are found in Shan State. Zo, Pa'O, Palaung, and Kokang zones feature secessionist conflicts, but these have diminished as rebels have been co-opted as militias (Buchanan 2017). The only zone not in Shan State, Naga Zone, has two secessionist movements connected to co-ethnics in India. Myanmar has recognized two dozen former ethnic insurgent groups as Border Guard Forces (BGFs), militias used to fight secessionism (Buchanan 2017). Studying secessionism in Myanmar is also complicated by multiparty ceasefires, with some groups signing on (and thus freezing their struggles), some refusing to cease hostilities, and others joining ceasefires and then returning to the battlefield.

In Rakhine State, ethnic Arakanese led a decades-long secessionist struggle under various organizations, including the Arakan Liberation Army (ALA). The conflict diminished in the 1980s, with the ALA accepting a ceasefire in 2012, at which point it became embroiled in anti-Muslim violence. Other Arakanese organizations have been co-opted as BGFs. Operating in Kachin State, the

Arakan Army (AA) remains active, although it has ostensibly shifted its goals toward autonomy. Meanwhile, secessionism has also diminished in Mon areas. Ethnic Mon communities mobilized powerful secessionist movements in the 1960s, which declined in the 1980s in part because their territory is proximate to ethnically Burmese areas. The New Mon State Party (NMSP) refused to become a BGF but is inactive after various peace agreements. Ethnic Shan communities have featured powerful secessionist movements, although many have fragmented and aligned with the state. In 2005, Burmese forces defeated the Shan State National Army (SSNA), with remaining rebels joining the Shan State Army (SSA). Several factions of the SSA-North became BGFs in the 2000s, although some SSA-North rebel forces remain active.

The three largest secessionist groups in Myanmar are found in eastern border areas: Kayin (Karen), Kayah (Karenni), and Kachin states. Among the first major secessionist groups in Myanmar was the Karen National Union (KNU) and its military wing, the Karen National Liberation Army. Based in Kayin State along the Thai border, Karen secessionists have fought for independence for decades. Their power diminished in the 1990s when Buddhist Karen created a splinter organization and aligned with the government against the KNU (Thawnghmung 2012, 117). The weakened KNU fought on, then signed cease-fires in 2012 and 2015. In Kayah State, also along the Thai border, the Karenni National Progressive Party (KNPP) and its armed wing were established in 1957. After decades of secessionist conflict, the KNPP signed a ceasefire in 2012. Perhaps the largest active secessionist movement is the Kachin Independence Organization (KIO). Established in 1961, the KIO is based out of remote Kachin State, bordering China in the north. It remains dedicated to independence, with major clashes in 2011 and 2015. The KIO is a leading member of a rebel coalition that has engaged in peace talks through 2020.

Among Southeast Asian secessionist conflicts, those in Myanmar are notable for their considerable duration, with many lasting for over half a century, as well as for rebels' ability to control territory in Myanmar's mountainous north. The conflicts are also notable for their remarkable complexity, with factions, side-switching, state co-optation programs, surrenders, and various ceasefires making for an exceptionally complicated landscape. It is likely that this complexity undermines the ability of any one state or group to attain independence, but it may also make the military unable to attain victory and control minority regions.

It is difficult, and perhaps foolish, to suggest that any given secessionist movement is ever defeated. A specific organization may be defeated or co-opted, but ethnic grievances and a desire to separate can remain, with secessionism suppressed or remaining dormant until times of crisis. This durability makes secessionist insurgencies different from revolutionary conflicts in Southeast Asia. Although class-based grievances endure, these do not easily translate into violent collective action in the absence of revolutionary vanguard organizations. Secessionism has a way of recurring, as collective memories of statehood and injustice motivate new generations to mobilize. This should not, however, suggest that secessionism is entirely intractable. More than revolutionary conflicts, secessionism is amenable to compromise.

3.4 Compromise: Autonomy

While it may be difficult to meet halfway on calls for national revolution and redistribution of wealth, secessionist movements often shift their demands from complete independence to self-government, given the right conditions. For this to occur, rebel groups must be cohesive, somewhat accountable, and capable of governance. If secessionists are riddled with factions or undertake predatory violence against civilians, their ability to govern is questionable and autonomy may fail. Another necessary component is a willing, credible host state. Coming to the table with rebel groups is a dangerous step for national authorities, as doing so may legitimize and unify rebels, provide opportunities for rebels to regroup, and encourage other secessionist groups (Kaplow 2016). State leaders sometimes do not negotiate in good faith, using talks to deflect international pressure or to gain intelligence regarding rebel groups; even good-faith efforts are sometimes undermined by hardliners. However, if secessionist insurgents and state authorities can engage in meaningful talks, secessionism can be overcome through compromise – self-government through territorial autonomy.

A prominent case of resolving secessionism through compromise is Aceh, Indonesia. Aceh has a long history as an independent sultanate, a center of Islamic learning, and anti-colonial resistance (Reid 2005). The secessionist conflict formally began in 1976, when local elites, sidelined from provincial development, proclaimed independence and formed the Free Aceh Movement (GAM). The first uprising was defeated, leading many to believe that Acehnese secessionism was finished by the mid-1980s. However, GAM returned in 1989. Their second uprising triggered a military crackdown, with Indonesian forces committing widespread human rights abuses against a shadowy secessionist threat (Kell 1995). When the New Order collapsed in 1997–8, resentment toward Indonesia boiled over, and the East Timor referendum signaled an opportunity. GAM finally had public support and became a major secessionist threat.

Against a weakened Indonesian state, GAM developed into a powerful secessionist movement. GAM championed Acehnese ethno-nationalism, downplaying Islam while promoting historical myths and symbols. Its leaders created history books, nationalist theatre and opera, a calendar, symbols including a flag and coat of arms, and much more. As Aspinall (2009, 54) notes, GAM's historiography represents "a textbook case – indeed, almost a *parody* – of ethnohistory." GAM founder Hasan di Tiro expounded the virtues of the Acehnese race and blood, Aceh's historical statehood, the "illegal" transfer of sovereignty to Indonesia, and Aceh's rich, superior culture. He suggests that the "Achehnese nation" (GAM insisted on spelling it "Acheh") faces a crisis under "indonesia" (GAM refused to capitalize "Indonesia"): "This is why we are here, to organize a resistance for the survival of our people, our language, our culture, our religion, our custom, our way of life, and our right to live as a sovereign people" (di Tiro 1984, 45). Part of this nationalism meant amplifying differences with Indonesia and Aceh's minorities. GAM leaders long derided ethnic Javanese as "an effeminate race with infantile culture" (di Tiro 1979, 4). In late 1999, GAM began targeting Aceh's Javanese communities in an effort to cleanse their homeland, stoking communal conflict within the secessionist insurgency (Barter 2015b).

Meanwhile, a now democratic Indonesia was regrouping and promising reforms. In 2000, President Wahid made the important step of meeting with rebel leaders. This led to a brief ceasefire followed by a more substantial agreement in 2002. Indonesia also granted autonomy to Aceh, although the rebels were excluded from this newfound power (Miller 2008). Peace talks fell apart in 2003, with Indonesian military offensives claiming more civilian lives and weakening GAM, whose momentum waned as it became clear that independence was not imminent. In December 2004, a devastating earthquake and tsunami struck Aceh, killing over 100,000 people. This accelerated new peace efforts, bringing global attention and international funding to a province tired of suffering. GAM dropped its unconditional demand for independence while Indonesia allowed the rebels to form a political party and offered a revamped autonomy arrangement. Acehnese secessionism killed approximately 20,000 people, displacing and traumatizing many more (KKR 2019). However, the conflict seems to have ended in compromise, as secessionist rebels shifted their goals when presented with a sincere opportunity to govern their territory within Indonesia (see Section 5).

Secessionism in the southern Philippines has also seemingly been managed through compromise, although this case is more complex. The island of Mindanao has seen extensive Christian migration and features several Muslim (Moro) ethnic communities affiliated with different armed groups. Precolonial sultanates long resisted Spanish colonizers and, under American rule, Mindanao was governed separately (Hawkins 2013). As Americans granted

Filipinos greater power in the 1930s, one effect was growing Christian migration to Mindanao, producing communal violence in the 1960s. When it came to light that the Philippine government killed Muslim recruits in an abortive attempt to destabilize Malaysia, an event known as the Jabidah Massacre, Moros were outraged (Aljunied & Curaming 2012). After President Marcos declared martial law in 1972, student leaders formed the Moro National Liberation Front (MNLF). MNLF leaders were initially influenced by communism, speaking of class and exploitation, while also framing Filipino Muslims as a nation. Kaufman (2011, 945) analyzes how the MNLF came to frame violence in Mindanao as an anti-colonial struggle on behalf of an oppressed nation. MNLF leader Nur Misuari was initially influenced by communist movements, criticizing pro-state Moro elites. The MNLF expanded quickly in the 1970s, although failed peace talks and political maneuvering by President Marcos slowed its growth. The MNLF soon fragmented "as the different tribes within the Muslim community came into conflict with one another" (Abinales 2000, 2). While the MNLF was strongest in Sulu among ethnic Tausug, the newly formed Moro Islamic Liberation Front (MILF) was more religious and represented ethnic Maguindanao in Mindanao. Ethnic divisions thus undermined the idea of a Moro nation.

Philippine People Power and the restoration of democracy in 1986 presented opportunities for peace in Mindanao. President Aquino granted some autonomy to Muslim Mindanao in 1989, and in 1996 President Ramos signed a peace agreement with the MNLF. In 1998, President Estrada expanded the conflict, destroying the MILF's self-governing camps and displacing thousands. The rise of the Abu Sayyaf Group (ASG), a criminal terrorist organization based in Sulu, complicated peace efforts and drew American involvement. As the MILF has moderated its demands for independence, the major issue has been "ancestral domain" – Moro lands now occupied by settlers. In the past century, Moros have gone from two-thirds to one-quarter of Mindanao's population, with Christians settling along roadways and dominating the agricultural sector. Other complicating factors include the position of indigenous Lumad communities (Paredes 2015), violent clan feuding, criminal violence, and rebel splinter groups. Despite these challenges, MILF signed the Comprehensive Agreement on the Bangsamoro in 2014 and agreed to lay down their arms. It is difficult to see the conflict as completely resolved, especially with ongoing criminal, terrorist, and communal violence, but it appears that secessionism may be no more, at least for now, as the main rebel groups have accepted autonomy.

The presence of compromise in the form of territorial autonomy should not suggest that a secessionist conflict is extinguished. Again, secessionism has a way of enduring and recurring. Autonomy thus represents a form of conflict management rather than of enduring resolution. This said, meaningful autonomy has a highly successful track record (Barter 2018). It is generally only when host states rescind autonomy and reassert centralized control that secessionist conflict is most likely to recur, as the loss of autonomy is added to grievances held by minority communities against the state.

3.5 Conclusions

This section has surveyed Southeast Asia's many secessionist conflicts, including one case of successful independence, various unresolved cases, and two examples of compromise. A form of insurgency and ethnic conflict, secessionism seeks independence for ethnic minority nations. Like revolutionary conflicts, secessionist conflicts are insurgencies, featuring organized rebel groups that aspire to become governments. Just as revolutionary struggles contain ethnic dimensions, secessionist conflicts also feature elements of class and revolutionary aspirations. Early GAM statements spoke of Aceh being "at the feet of multinationals to be raped" while corporations "buy and sell us in international market" (di Tiro 1984, 75). The MNLF was formed by leftist student leaders who initially approached Moro concerns in terms of class (Stark 2003, 202). Secessionist views of class exploitation, though, typically follow ethnic group lines, depicting dominant ethnic groups as exploiting minority nations.

Table 2 lists secessionist conflicts in Southeast Asia, summarizing the main combatants, duration, outcome, and casualties. Again, casualty data is not intended to be definitive. These estimates nonetheless provide a sense of shifting conflict intensity. Casualty rates in secessionist insurgencies are typically lower than in revolutionary insurgencies because several communist conflicts involved external actors and occurred over more expansive territories. Secessionist conflicts are geographically limited to minority areas, where rebel forces often attempt to defend their ethnic group.

As Figure 3 shows, revolutionary and secessionist insurgencies feature similar historical arcs but with some key differences. For revolutionary conflicts, casualties hovered in the range of 30,000 for many years, with casualties for the more numerous secessionist conflicts rising to just over 10,000. Secessionist violence peaked later than revolutionary violence, with early conflicts in Maluku and Myanmar joined by Patani, Mindanao, Aceh, Papua, and Timor from the late 1960s. Secessionist violence also declined later than revolutionary insurgencies, diminishing in the 1990s and 2000s. Declining intensity in secessionist conflicts is not as sharp as for revolutionary conflicts, as several have diminished, but remain unresolved with occasional clashes. Clearly, though, secessionist violence has declined.

Table 2 Major secessionist conflicts in Southeast Asia

Conflict	Insurgents	Country	Duration	Outcome	Casualties
Arakan	ALA, AA, others	Myanmar	1948–94	Diminished	≈30,000[1]
Karen	KNU	Myanmar	1949–	Ongoing	≈15,000–70,000[2]
Mon	NMSP, others	Myanmar	1949–96	Diminished	≈10,000[3]
Maluku	RMS	Indonesia	1950–63	Defeated	≈1,000
Karenni	KNPP	Myanmar	1957–	Ongoing	≈5,000[4]
Shan	SSA, others	Myanmar	1959–12	Diminished	≈20,000–100,000[5]
Papua	OPM, others	Indonesia	1963–	Ongoing	≈20,000[6]
Kachin	KIO	Myanmar	1960–	Ongoing	≈20,000–70,000[7]
Patani	PULO, BRN, others	Thailand	1968–	Ongoing	≈11,000[8]
Mindanao	MNLF, MILF	Philippines	1972–2014+	Autonomy	≈40,000[9]
East Timor	Fretilin	Indonesia	1976–2000	Independence	≈100,000[10]
Aceh	GAM	Indonesia	1976–2005	Autonomy	≈10,000–20,000[11]

1. PRIO estimates 1,100–44,000 casualties (1948–94).
2. PRIO estimates 15,000–70,000 casualties (1949–2008). COW combines Karen secessionism CPB revolutionary conflict (for 1983–8) and combines the Karen and Karenni conflicts in the 1990s.
3. PRIO estimates 500–16,000 casualties (1948–96).
4. PRIO provides estimates for four years (1957, 1992, 1996, and 2005), estimating 25–999 casualties/year.
5. PRIO estimates 9,000–110,000 casualties (1959–2008).
6. PRIO estimates 18,000 casualties (1965–78). Some sources cite "official estimates" of 150,000 casualties (1963–83), although the source of this claim is unclear (Crocombe 2007, 287).
7. PRIO estimates 15,000–93,000 casualties (1949–92).
8. PRIO estimates 2,000 casualties (2003–8). Deep South Watch estimates 7,000 casualties (2004–19), with about 3,000 casualties during the 1970s.
9. PRIO estimates 12,500–110,000 casualties (1970–2008). COW estimates 40,000 casualties. Capuno cites estimates of 7,000 casualties for 2011–16.
10. PRIO estimates 15,000–101,000 casualties (1975–98). East Timor's Commission for Reception, Truth and Reconciliation (CAVR) estimates 100,000 casualties.
11. PRIO estimates 4,500 casualties, with a range of 1,376–18,703 (1990–2005). COW estimates 6,000 casualties. Aceh's Truth and Reconciliation

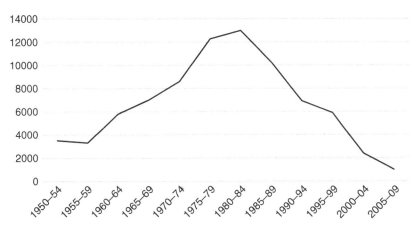

Figure 3 Casualty estimates, Southeast Asian secessionist conflicts
Source: PRIO 2012, coded as five-year averages

It is possible that the rise and decline of secessionist violence is related to trends in revolutionary conflict. Secessionist struggles were often inspired by revolutionary conflicts, also benefiting materially from the availability of weapons and states focusing on communist violence. Many human rights grievances fueling secessionism were rooted in how states responded to communist threats, through more centralized, authoritarian, aggressive, and development-driven regimes. As states defeated communist insurgencies, secessionists were faced with fewer allies and weapons networks, as well as more focused and, eventually, less violent states. The interrelationship of communist and secessionist decline is evident along the Thai-Malay border, as the defeat of communist rebels weakened Patani secessionists and Thai authorities applied similar amnesty and development programs that had worked against the CPT.

Just as revolutionary conflicts are fading, so too are secessionist conflicts. No new secessionist conflicts have emerged in the region since the 1970s. While some minorities could develop a new sense of national consciousness in the future, it is unlikely that large new secessionist movements will form. The number of cases has diminished partly because secessionists have achieved or shifted their goals, but the majority of secessionist conflicts have declined in intensity without entirely fading away. Even among those that have been overcome through autonomy, recurrence is always possible. In the 1980s, experts suggested that the Aceh conflict was over, with economic development bringing Aceh within Indonesian networks (see King & Rasjid 1988, 921), only for it to return a few years later. Similarly, commentators proclaimed that the Patani conflict was peacefully resolved in the 1990s (Rahimmula 2003).

Secessionist insurgencies are ethnic conflicts, and crises or missteps by national leaders can trigger sudden recurrence. Fresh abuses or loss of self-government can reawaken the cause of independence. We should thus be reluctant to consign secessionist violence to Southeast Asian history.

4 Communal Conflicts

In July 1964, thousands of Singaporean Malays had gathered to celebrate an Islamic holiday. During the festivities, a series of fiery speeches sparked clashes between Malay and Chinese youths, unleashing communal violence that had been building for years. Dozens were killed and hundreds injured. The nature of the violence was shocking because it was fought not by trained combatants but by members of neighboring communities. In communal riots, violence can be highly symbolic and personal. According to one participant, "some Chinese use the pork to throw ... The Chinese during the procession slaughtered the Malay lah, so we retaliate after that" (qtd in Cheng 2001, 440). Rumors circulated that rioters threw pork at Muslims and threw beef at Hindus. Malays destroyed Chinese storefronts and shrines, while also targeting Chinese women. Violence flared up again in 1969, with communal tensions partly responsible for Singapore resisting democracy, which was framed by leaders as destabilizing. These communal riots are among the most important events in Singaporean history.

This section provides an overview of communal conflicts across Southeast Asia. After a brief conceptual discussion, it details ethnic riots, pogroms, and migratory conflicts, for each discussing their logic and providing examples. The discussion is organized by sub-types, not by conflict outcome. Communal conflicts tend to flare over a few days or weeks, then decline and flicker, perhaps recurring months or years later. This makes communal conflicts different from revolutionary or secessionist insurgencies. Generally lacking clear outcomes, communal conflicts do not involve the sort of temporal arcs we see elsewhere. Another key point made throughout this section concerns the role of the state, as political interests often lie behind seemingly spontaneous clashes.

4.1 Communal Conflict

Although a broad term, communal conflicts refer to "violent conflict between non-state groups that are organized along a shared communal identity" (Elfversson & Brosché 2012). Alongside secessionist conflicts, communal conflicts are forms of ethnic conflict. In most communal conflicts, ethnic identity demarcates the sides involved, with combatants emphasizing ethnic differences and engaging in ethnically potent acts of symbolic violence.

Collective insecurities, which may be amplified by elites, may lead ordinary people to believe that violence is legitimate or necessary.

While both are forms of ethnic conflict, secessionism and communal conflicts vary in four key respects. One difference is spatial: secessionism requires the presence of territorially concentrated minorities, typically in peripheral, 'separable' regions. Communal conflicts, however, unfold where ethnic groups are interspersed, with communities living side by side. Studies of ethnic conflict have long noted the importance of spatial settlement in the creation and resolution of ethnic conflicts (Coakley 1993). The same grievances and fears that fuel secessionism in one location may thus fuel communal violence in another, with distinct settlement patterns generating different types of violence. Communal conflicts require proximity, often developing in urban areas or migration sites. Violence typically leads to some degree of bifurcation, with both sides separating to some extent but remaining in the same region. Secessionism is not feasible when groups are interspersed, which is precisely why states encourage migration to secessionist areas, essentially transforming secessionist conflicts into communal ones. This is why secessionists often target migrants and criticize states for internal colonialism. The spatial nature of communal conflicts is especially important for conflict management, as communities affected by violence must live alongside one another after the conflict fades.

A second difference is that secessionist conflicts are a form of insurgency against the state, whereas communal conflicts are fought between communities. Secessionism thus involves trained rebel groups, while communal conflicts are more amorphous, involving semiprofessional and untrained fighters. Those involved in violence are, in a broad sense, "civilians," generally lacking formal training, uniforms, modern weapons, or clear command structures. Because they are fought by such irregular forces, communal conflicts may feature especially shocking forms of violence, aiming at symbolic dominance of the other side. This may entail intense sexual violence, asserting biological supremacy (Krause 2020). They may also involve attacks on religious symbols, asserting cosmological power. Some examples of symbolic attacks in communal conflicts include Muslims killing cows in India, noisy processions disrupting Muslim religious services, throwing animal blood on religious sites, disrespecting holy texts, occupying and destroying sacred spaces, and more (Brubaker & Laitin 1998, 445).

One implication of communal conflicts being intergroup rather than traditional insurgencies relates to the role of the state, a third major difference between secessionist and communal conflicts. Violence in communal conflicts may appear random and unplanned, with ordinary people losing control.

Although the state is not a central belligerent as it is in insurgencies, it remains intimately involved in communal conflicts. The state may be relatively neutral, seeking to manage conflicts and promote peace. Alternatively, the state may lack the capacity to manage conflict or may allow conflicts to occur because doing so serves the political interests of state leaders. State officials may favor co-ethnics or other loyal populations, perhaps aiding state-sponsored migrants. Different parts of the state may also be drawn into communal conflicts, with various levels of government and agencies intertwined with a particular side, sometimes resulting in parts of the state fighting other parts. Politicians may be responsible for communal violence as they stoke fears, but may or may not be entirely in control of the conflicts they helped create.

Fourth, communal conflicts have distinctive temporal dynamics. As discussed in previous sections, revolutionary and secessionist insurgencies are sustained conflicts with distinctive temporal trends. Communal conflicts often unfold in brief, violent flares before order is restored, and, instead of being common to a particular era, they unfold at moments of crisis and regime change. These moments are sometimes referred to as "critical junctures" – moments in which political systems are renegotiated. In his study of ethnic conflict in Indonesia, Bertrand (2004, 20) argues that such political crises are crucial to explaining the timing and conditions of ethnic conflicts. So, while the preceding analysis suggests that revolutionary and secessionist conflicts are slowly being overcome in Southeast Asia, communal conflicts represent a perennial threat, especially in ethnically diverse societies.

Communal conflict is an especially broad category, containing many forms and logics. In his study of violence in Indonesia, Sidel (2006) differentiates between riots, pogroms, and jihad. He sees riots giving way to larger-scale pogroms as the state lost control, then a shift to religious violence. My focus is slightly different, as "jihad" is a problematic concept, threatening to essentialize Islamic violence, while migratory violence should be discussed as its own category. A riot is a form of violent public disorder, pitching people against rival groups or the state. Horowitz (2001, 1) defines a riot as "an intense, sudden, though not necessarily wholly unplanned, lethal attack by civilian members of one ethnic group on civilian members of another ethnic group, the victims chosen because of their group membership." Riots tend to be brief, flaring for a few days or hours, sometimes recurring in the near future. A pogrom is in essence a sustained riot involving unequal sides, with the stronger group aiming at cleansing others. In pogroms, the state encourages, allows, or is unable to halt violence, thus its greater scale (Brass 1996). Migratory conflicts, meanwhile, are communal conflicts involving migrant and native groups, with natives violently resisting encroachment (Weiner 1978). These three forms of communal conflict overlap and are not exhaustive, but this categorization is useful in understanding intergroup conflicts.

4.2 Ethnic Riots

Southeast Asia has experienced numerous ethnic riots in the postcolonial era, far too many to discuss here individually. Some of the most notable, publicized cases were in Malaysia and Singapore, countries whose histories of riots shape modern politics. The colonial origins of these riots are undeniable. In the nineteenth century, the British wanted cheap sources of labor for mines and plantations. Because the British had agreed with sultans not to interfere in Malay society, and because they saw Malay workers as unreliable, colonial authorities recruited laborers from southern India and southern China instead. Bringing together groups with different cultures, languages, religions, and economic roles generated tensions, especially as migrants were uncertain if they could stay and native Malays felt sidelined. Singapore suffered anti-Christian riots as well as violence between Chinese clans in the 1850s, leaving hundreds dead. By the early 1900s, Malays were approximately 50 percent of the peninsula's population and were at risk of being minorities in their homeland.

In 1963, Malaya merged with Singapore, Sabah, and Sarawak to form Malaysia. However, the inclusion of Chinese-majority Singapore, which had well-organized, largely Chinese political parties, challenged Malay dominance. As noted in the introduction to this section, the 1964 riots between Malay Muslims and ethnic Chinese featured shocking ethnic symbolism that corroded community ties. The 1964 Race Riots in Singapore left dozens dead and several hundred injured (Mauzy & Milne 2002, 222). Facing ethnic riots and Singapore's ruling party challenging Malaysian leaders, Singapore agreed to leave Malaysia in 1965. More riots followed in 1969, when the electoral decline of Malaysia's ruling Alliance led to Chinese celebrations and Malay retaliation, resulting in hundreds of deaths (Clutterbuck 1985, 289).

Southeast Asian countries have experienced numerous riots against ethnic Chinese and Indian minorities. All Southeast Asian countries have seen violence directed at Chinese minorities, a successful entrepreneurial minority throughout the region, whom scholars sometimes compare to European Jewish communities, given the ethnic resentment and prejudice both groups have faced over time (Chirot & Reid 2011). Brunei saw attacks against Chinese communities in 1962 and still refuses to grant citizenship to many ethnically Chinese residents. As explained, Cambodian and Vietnamese communists targeted ethnic Chinese. In post-reunification Vietnam, the VCP demanded that ethnic Chinese naturalize and assimilate, forcibly relocating ethnic Chinese from border areas. During wars with Cambodia and China, "the campaign against all ethnic Chinese in Vietnam was stepped up and became nationwide in scope" (Chang 1982, 204). In 1978, authorities stood by as Ho Chi Minh City saw anti-Chinese riots, generating hundreds of thousands of refugees. In post-colonial Burma, authorities nationalized Chinese businesses and banned Chinese education. Burmese rioters attacked Chinese schools in 1967, leaving dozens dead (Fan 2012, 238). In response to government policy and violence, tens of thousands of ethnic Chinese fled Burma.

Indonesia has a tragic history of violence against ethnic Chinese communities. After independence, the Chinese were often targeted in anti-communist and anti-capitalist violence. In Java, militias targeted Chinese traders, destroying Chinese stores and killing several thousand ethnic Chinese (Somers-Heidhues 2012). Contrary to popular belief, ethnic Chinese were not the primary targets of the 1965 politicide. Cribb (2001, 233) notes that "Chinese Indonesians have been subject to discrimination, harassment, and occasional pogroms for at least the last 250 years. In 1965–6, however, few Chinese were targeted." He explains that most anti-communist killings were rural, while Indonesian laws forced ethnic Chinese into urban areas. This saved them from the worst violence in the 1960s, but not from urban riots at the end of the New Order in 1997–8. In Jakarta, "crowds attacked, destroyed, and burned shops, supermarkets, department stores, goods, and other property owned by Chinese Indonesians" (Sidel 2006, 1). For Bertrand (2004), by 1998, "anti-Chinese disturbances had become a regular feature of the political landscape." As a result, I discuss the culmination of the 1998 riots in terms of pogroms.

Ethnic Indians have also been subject to periodic violence, with Myanmar seeing extensive attacks against its Indian minorities. This history is rooted in the British decision to rule Burma as part of India, enabling the migration of Indian bureaucrats, traders, and moneylenders. Burmese rioters attacked Indians on several occasions in the 1930s, leaving hundreds dead, thousands injured, and businesses destroyed (Egreteau 2011, 39). When Ne Win seized power in 1962, the military nationalized Indian businesses and tolerated anti-Indian riots, leading to several deaths and hundreds of thousands of Indians fleeing Burma. In the following decades, anti-Indian sentiment shifted to become more religious, specifically targeting Muslims. Anti-Muslim riots have unfolded across the country since the 1990s. In 2001, anti-Muslim pamphlets referred to Muslim plans to destroy Buddhism and the Burmese race, sparking riots that left hundreds dead.

Anti-Muslim violence has been most intense in Rakhine State, home to Rohingya Muslim minorities near Bangladesh. Despite being previously recognized as Burmese citizens, the Rohingya were stripped of citizenship in the 1982 Nationality Law. With army support, anti-Rohingya violence expanded in the late 1990s. In the 2010s, anti-Rohingya violence expanded dramatically. In 2012, rumors of Muslim men raping Buddhist girls sparked riots in Rakhine State that killed over 200 and displaced 10,000 (Walton & Hayward 2014, 7). Anti-Rohingya violence has interacted with smaller riots across the country, generating an intense Islamophobia. As with anti-Chinese violence in Indonesia, we must see anti-Muslim violence in Myanmar as an ethnic pogrom.

At the end of this section, Table 3 provides a summary of communal riots in Southeast Asia. This is an abbreviated list, with dozens of smaller riots leaving hundreds injured, displaced, and impoverished. It is useful to note the clustering of ethnic riots, speaking to their brief but chronic nature. Riots tend to explode in one locale, simmer down, and then be triggered anew by a seemingly random event. This makes it difficult to know whether to see them as multiple events or as part of a single larger conflict. Riots are often smaller in scale than other forms of conflict, but they are also some of the most common forms of ethnic conflicts in Southeast Asia.

4.3 Pogroms

At a certain point, as authorities prove unwilling or unable to contain a riot – or when authorities benefit from its expansion – it becomes a pogrom. Pogroms are sustained, asymmetrical episodes of communal violence. They consist of assaults by a dominant community against a more vulnerable rival, often with state support. While riots appear chaotic, the sustained, structured nature of pogroms demand political involvement. As noted by Brass (1996, 10), ethnic prejudices and tensions do not automatically result in riots or pogroms; instead, sustained patterns of unrest are fueled by "identifiable persons and interests." Pogroms are forms of ethnic cleansing. Just as sustained riots at some point must be understood as pogroms, over time pogroms become genocide, in which the culpability of the state becomes increasingly clear.

Numerous instances of violence in Southeast Asia could be seen as ethnic pogroms. In Cambodia, the 1975–9 Khmer Rouge "Killing Fields" are often referred to as a genocide due to the staggering volume of deaths. The UN (1948) defines genocide as violence "committed with intent to destroy, in whole or in part, a national, ethnical, racial or religious group." Genocide thus involves efforts to eliminate a specific community. Cambodia saw ethnic Khmers carrying out extreme violence and mass murder of other ethnic Khmers. However, the Khmer Rouge also disproportionately targeted ethnic minorities, namely Chinese, Vietnamese, and Cham Muslims (Kiernan 2002, 460). The Khmer Rouge reign thus included ethnic pogroms as part of a broader state-led mass killing.

Another Southeast Asian pogrom was the anti-Chinese violence in Indonesia during the fall of Suharto. Chinese businessmen were symbols of the corrupt New Order government and were thus scapegoated by poorer Indonesians and aspiring elites. In 1998, cities across the country experienced widespread anti-Chinese violence. Of course, the rich businessmen connected to Suharto could afford security or to flee, with poorer Chinese feeling the wrath of attackers, who looted and burned Chinese stores and homes. There were 150 reported rapes targeting Chinese women, with the actual volume of sexual violence drastically underreported. The Jakarta riots left over 1,500 dead, including many rioters trapped inside burning buildings (Sidel 2006, 121). It is widely understood that the pogrom was not random: many rioters appeared to be off-duty soldiers, and leaders were scapegoating Chinese businessmen. For Siegel (1998, 87), Jakarta residents recall trucks shuttling in well-equipped rioters, as locals believed that politicians and the military organized violence against the Chinese to demonstrate a need for order. Over the next two decades, Indonesian leaders worked to repair relations with ethnic Chinese; however, anti-Chinese sentiment again surfaced in 2016. In the Jakarta gubernatorial race, Islamic groups and opposition candidates used anti-Chinese slurs against the popular Christian Chinese incumbent, Ahok, who was later found guilty of a trumped-up charge of blasphemy. Violence and renewed tensions in 2016 forced ethnic Chinese Indonesians to relive the horrors of 1998.

Anti-Muslim violence in Myanmar also escalated from riots into pogroms. In the 2000s, we could see anti-Muslim violence as riots, with Buddhist communities attacking Muslim communities. But the scale soon expanded, with military and state support for the violence. Far from preaching peace, parts of the Buddhist Sangha have fueled anti-Muslim violence. Radical Buddhist groups such as Ma Ba Tha and the 969 Movement, especially the extremist monk Ashin Wirathu, have spread conspiracy theories and incited crowds to attack Muslims (Bertrand & Pelletier 2017). In late 2016, Buddhist gangs renewed attacks on the Rohingya, this time with military support. Violence expanded in August 2017, again perpetrated by Buddhist mobs supported by state security forces. The pogroms killed an estimated 7,000 people, with entire villages destroyed and over a million people displaced (MSF 2017). The UN criticized these "crimes against humanity," with the Secretary General referring to the Rohingya as "one of, if not the, most discriminated people in the world" (Guterres 2018). Violence against Rohingya as well as other Muslims in

Myanmar represents ethnic cleansing, a pogrom that developed after years of riots.

4.4 Migratory Conflicts

Another form of ethnic conflict involves nativist violence against migrants. Of course, many ethnic conflicts feature elements of nativism against perceived migrants. This is true of secessionism, in which militants typically claim sovereignty over their ethnic homelands. GAM in Aceh spoke against Javanese migration as a plot to "Indonesianize" their province; rebels in Patani have targeted Thai Buddhist migrants; and the rise of secessionism in Mindanao was partly a response to state-supported Christian migration. Although resisting migration to their homeland, secessionists rarely speak in terms of indigenous rights. In many communal conflicts, such as anti-Chinese violence in Jakarta or anti-Rohingya violence in Myanmar, perpetrators frame their victims as foreign and say they are defending their country against external threats. However, these cases are different than migratory conflicts. Chinese in Jakarta were hardly recent migrants, having lived in the city for centuries. Although they have co-ethnics in Bangladesh and a history of cross-border mobility, Rohingya are not migrants.

Research on migratory violence developed from studies of violent communal conflicts in South Asia, with such conflicts referred to as Sons of the Soil conflicts (Weiner 1978). Early studies have produced a spate of research to help us better understand connections between migration, autochthony, and violence (Côté and Mitchell 2017). The idea of conflicts being waged by "Sons of the Soil" is problematic. For one, the term is gendered, although this may reflect gendered patterns of migration as well as violence (Côté & Huang 2020). Further, it is unclear if the concept of Sons of the Soil conflict refers only to natives instigating violence or also includes migrant attacks against natives. After all, powerful host communities may abuse poor landless migrants, but it is also possible that state-supported internal migrants may colonize indigenous territories – the migrant or host may enjoy a position of power, depending on circumstances (Barter & Ascher 2019). For such reasons, I refer to migratory violence when referring to these conflicts.

Southeast Asia features several migratory conflicts; here I focus on three Indonesian cases. Indonesia has featured several such conflicts, partly a product of its immense scale and ethnic diversity but also due to its highly mobile population. Many Indonesian ethnic communities feature *rantau* traditions, in which youths are expected to leave home in search of education, spirituality, wealth, and adventure. These traditions have been amplified by the state, as

Dutch colonial and then Indonesian officials relocated millions of people from densely populated inner islands, especially Java, to sparsely populated outer islands (Riwanto 2013). Given the dramatic scale of transmigration as well as the country's many migratory conflicts, it is often assumed that state-led transmigration caused violence. This is not entirely accurate, though, as Javanese transmigrants have not typically been involved in migratory conflicts, even when they live in areas with active anti-migrant conflicts. Instead, conflicts mostly developed from non-state, spontaneous migration, especially Muslim traders moving to towns across the eastern islands (Barter & Côté 2015).

The following discussion focuses on three Indonesian migratory conflicts: Kalimantan, Poso (Sulawesi), and Maluku. All three are similar in that they involved native Christians clashing with migrant Muslim groups (as well as native Muslims). In all three, the migrants involved in violence were not official transmigrants but instead spontaneous migrants. The conflicts varied in the importance of indigenous themes, the relative power of native Christians, and the roles of outside actors.

The conflicts in Kalimantan consisted of three major and several smaller incidents. The island of Borneo/Kalimantan features Muslim Malays living along the coasts and various Christian-majority indigenous communities, often known collectively as "Dayak," in the interior. In the late 1990s, Indonesian Kalimantan saw conflicts between indigenous Dayak Christians and ethnic Madurese Muslims, who migrated to West and Central Kalimantan to work in the timber industry and trade in towns. In late 1996, before the Asian Financial Crisis and the fall of Suharto, ethnic clashes in West Kalimantan involved Dayak attacks on Madurese communities, leaving nearly 500 dead (HRW 1997). The violence was a result of destructive forestry practices associated with the Madurese, a growing assertiveness of Dayak indigenous identity, and cultural frictions with Madurese Muslims. In the context of a falling New Order, violence again erupted in West Kalimantan in February 1999, specifically in the district of Sambas. This time, the conflict featured Malay Muslims attacking migrant Madurese Muslims, laying bare that Kalimantan's tensions were more about migration than religion.

In 2001, violence between Dayak and Madurese communities erupted in Central Kalimantan. In February, rumors of violence committed by Madurese youths cascaded into a conflict that killed 500 and displaced 100,000, with most victims being Madurese. The conflict involved rumors of Dayak headhunting, reviving colonial-era primitive stereotypes. Together, migratory conflicts in Kalimantan left thousands dead and hundreds of thousands displaced. The conflicts have been explained in terms of political jockeying amid national instability (Bertrand 2004), cultural differences, migration, indigenous cultural renewal, and legacies of Cold War violence (Davidson 2008). Clearly, Madurese were targeted for being migrants. It is striking that, in the aftermath of this migratory conflict, Madurese victims have been afforded little sympathy, as if being migrants justifies their persecution. Dayak communities even celebrated how their warriors destroyed the Madurese (Davidson 2008, 144).

Another migratory conflict erupted in 1998 and 2000 in the Poso district of Sulawesi, just east of Kalimantan. Sulawesi island has a distinct "K" shape, with the lower peninsulas home to powerful Bugis and Makassarese ethnic communities. These groups, along with the nearby Butonese, are collectively referred to as "BBM," known as successful and mobile Muslim traders. Meanwhile, the northern areas of Sulawesi are home to Christian communities favored by Dutch colonizers. Poso lies at the intersection, home to Muslim and Christian settlements. Sustained local migration and state-led transmigration resulted in a Muslim majority and, in the upheaval of Indonesian *reformasi*, degenerated into violence in 1998. Indonesian security forces sometimes halted violent incidents, whereas at other times they took sides and expanded the violence. Aragon (2001) explains that, in an ethnically charged context, communities responded to perceived affronts "with a pattern of multiplied revenge," a common feature in communal conflicts (Aragon 2001, 47). Over two years, the conflict killed over 1,000 and displaced hundreds of thousands (HRW 2002).

A third Indonesian migratory conflict unfolded around the same time just to the east, in the Maluku islands. The first clashes began on the island of Ambon. During the colonial era, the Dutch favored the Christian Ambonese in education and employment. As discussed in Section 3, South Maluku waged a brief secessionist insurgency as Indonesia became independent. Even after this, their educational advantages meant Ambonese were disproportionately represented in the Indonesian military and bureaucracy. The rise of a Muslim bureaucratic class across the country, population growth, and BBM in-migration undermined this status, leading to war in the context of decentralization and electoral competition. In January 1999, a clash between a Christian bus driver and Bugis youths sparked intercommunal fighting. Violence expanded into nearby islands, re-erupting in March and again in November. North Maluku then saw fighting between native communities and ethnic Makianese, who had been resettled there after a natural disaster. Clashes then spread to Ternate and Tidor, two Muslim-majority islands, with the sultan of Ternate sheltering Christian minorities. By April 2000, violence was complicated by the arrival of Laskar Jihad, a radical militia seeking to defend Muslims. Laskar Jihad enjoyed military training and advanced weaponry, attacking Christian villages (Sidel 2006, 184). Efforts to crack down on the militia were limited, as Laskar Jihad maintained good relations with parts of the Indonesian military. Over three years, over 5,000 were killed and hundreds of thousands were displaced (Davidson 2008, 5). The conflict died down as authorities regained control and took action against Laskar Jihad, although sporadic incidents would recur in the years to come.

4.5 Other Communal Conflicts

In addition to riots, pogroms, and migratory conflicts, other forms of communal conflicts have also taken lives across Southeast Asia. One is clan feuding, known as *rido* in the southern Philippines. Clan feuding is often overlooked as a form of violence, perhaps because it is seen as antiquated, reminiscent of Montagues and Capulets or Hatfields and McCoys. In many parts of the world, clan-based kinship ties remain the locus of politics and employment (see McCoy 2009). Clan ties are especially salient in remote highland regions beyond the reach of the state. In the absence of state authority, people often view security and justice in terms of self-help and as a collective enterprise: if one clan member is attacked, all are expected to respond. Clan-based violence is found throughout Southeast Asia, especially in the mountains of Myanmar, Mindanao, and Papua. Clan violence is low-intensity but chronic, with clans and clan alliances competing for economic and political advantage. It is estimated that hundreds die every year due to clan conflict in Papua (Reilly 2008, 15), with even more casualties in Mindanao (Torres 2014).

The effects of clan-based violence are amplified as they intersect with other forms of conflict. As Adam (2013) has argued, focusing on secessionist and communal conflicts obscures micro-level conflict dynamics linked to localized economic power and kinship. Papua, Mindanao, and northern Myanmar are home to secessionist conflicts, with a great deal of local fighting attributed to these higher-order political objectives. Secessionist conflict fuels clan violence, reducing the effectiveness of the state and increasing the availability of weapons. Clan feuds also drive secessionist conflict, with small, more personal clashes drawing in kin affiliated with armed groups. Sometimes what appears to be violence between rebels and the state is rooted in elopements, traffic accidents, or some act of disrespect between rival clans.

Just as clan feuds intersect with other forms of violence, it is important to acknowledge how communal conflicts exist within other forms of conflict. Secessionist conflict involves territorially concentrated ethnic minorities seeking independence. However, all regions contain minorities and many secessionist areas feature migrants, who are sometimes state-supported. As discussed, secessionist rebels typically lead nation-building efforts and attack local minorities. In Aceh, GAM undertook extensive violence against indigenous and Javanese migrant groups. Within the secessionist conflict there were patterns of intergroup violence, as non-Acehnese communities formed militias in response to rebel attacks (Barter 2013). In ethnically mixed districts such as Central and South Aceh, communal conflicts unfolded beneath the secessionist conflict. The intersection of communal and secessionist violence is also pronounced in Mindanao, where a century of internal migration has resulted in Christian majorities, making Moro independence no longer realistic. This has been acknowledged by rebel groups, who have instead worked for meaningful autonomy and to regain some lost territory. Throughout the secessionist conflict, as well as before and after it, southern Mindanao has seen communal violence between Moros, indigenous communities, and Christian migrants, a feature often overlooked as we focus on secessionism (Kaufman 2011).

4.6 Conclusions

This section has provided an overview of communal conflicts across Southeast Asia, discussing several different forms of such conflicts. Some are sudden riots, with brief flares of intense violence that recur in times of crisis as underlying tensions are left unresolved. As riots continue unchecked, and attain state support, they may become pogroms. Meanwhile, migratory conflicts involve clashes over territory and local power between migrant and native communities. All forms of communal conflict involve the state, even if the state is not a primary combatant. The state may establish peace and security, may be partial toward one side and intensify violence, or may be intersected by both sides. Communal conflicts are thus notable for how states are involved, not for their absence.

Some of Southeast Asia's many communal conflicts are summarized in Table 3, which lists the conflict, countries, major participants, approximate duration, and estimated casualties. Casualty estimates for communal conflicts are especially unreliable. Whereas estimates for revolutionary and secessionist insurgencies are based mostly on PRIO data, the smaller scale and uncertain horizons of communal conflict necessitate using estimates from the sources cited throughout this section. There are, no doubt, many cases absent from Table 3. Nevertheless, this summary allows us to visualize some important broader trends.

Estimates from Table 3 are visualized in Figure 4. Even with imperfect data, patterns of conflict fatalities are jarringly distinct from those found in revolutionary and secessionist insurgencies. Insurgencies show broad arcs of conflict escalation and decline. Communal conflicts are more sporadic and do not seem to be declining. They arise at moments of crisis and regime change, and thus

Table 3 Communal Conflicts in Southeast Asia

Conflict	Country	Participants	Duration	Casualties
Ethnic Riots				
Anti-Chinese violence	Indonesia	Javanese militias Chinese and Eurasians	1945–9	Thousands dead
Maria Hertogh Race Riots	Singapore	Malay Muslims Christians and Eurasians	December 1950	18 dead 173 injured
1964 race riots	Malaysia/ Singapore	Malay Muslims Chinese	July– September 1964	36 dead 560 injured
Anti-Chinese riots	Burma (Myanmar)	Burmese Chinese	June 1967	Dozens dead Hundreds injured
Anti-Indian riots	Burma (Myanmar)	Burmese Indians	1962	Several dead 300,000 displaced
1969 Race Riots	Singapore	Malay Muslims Chinese	May–June 1969	4 dead 80 injured
13 May Incident	Malaysia	Malay Muslims Chinese	May 1969	≈200 dead Hundreds injured
Anti-Chinese riots	Vietnam	Vietnamese Ethnic Chinese	1979	Hundreds dead
Anti-Chinese riots (various)	Indonesia	Various Indonesians Chinese	1994–7	Hundreds dead Thousands injured
Mandalay riots	Myanmar	Buddhists (Shan, Burmese) Muslims (Rohingya)	March 1997	3 dead Hundreds injured
Taungoo riots	Myanmar	Buddhists Muslims	May 2001	200 dead Thousands displaced

Table 3 (cont.)

Conflict	Country	Participants	Duration	Casualties
Rakhine State riots	Myanmar	Rakhine Buddhists Muslim Rohingya	June–October 2012	>200 dead 100,000 displaced
Anti-Muslim riots (various)	Myanmar	Buddhists Muslims	March 2013	≈80 dead Hundreds injured
Pogroms				
Anti-Vietnamese pogroms	Cambodia	Cambodians Ethnic Vietnamese	1970–2, 1970s	5,000 dead 200,000 displaced
Anti-Chinese pogroms	Indonesia	Muslims Ethnic Chinese	1998	>1,500 dead >100,000 injured >150 reported rapes
Anti-Muslim pogroms	Myanmar	Rakhine Buddhists Muslim Rohingya	2016–	>10,000 dead >400,000 injured 700,000 displaced
Migratory Conflicts				
Kalimantan	Indonesia	Dayak, Malay Madurese	1996–7 1999 (Sambas) 2001 (Sampit)	>5,000 dead >300,000 displaced
Poso	Indonesia	Native Protestant Christians Native Muslims Muslim Migrants	December 1998 April– June 2000	>1,000 dead >100,000 displaced
Maluku	Indonesia	Ambonese Christians Native Muslims Muslim Migrants	1999	>5,000 dead >200,000 displaced

Compiled from sources given throughout Section 4.

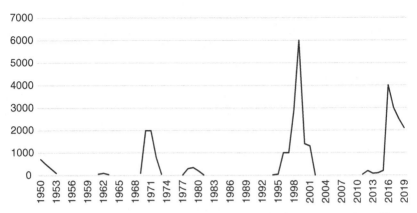

Figure 4 Casualty estimates, by year, Southeast Asian communal conflicts
Sources: Various throughout Section 4

they represent an ever-present threat in heterogeneous communities. In Figure 4, smaller peaks are due to communal violence in Malaysia, Singapore, and Indochina, whereas the larger peaks represent pogroms in Indonesia and Myanmar. Even more than insurgent conflicts, communal conflicts are notoriously difficult to manage and are rarely truly overcome. As a result, communal conflicts demand creative, sustained responses.

5 Peacebuilding

In December 2006, Aceh went to the polls. Although Indonesia began democratizing in 1999, Aceh was left mired in war, making this the province's democratization moment. The elections proceeded safely and fairly, returning a moderate rebel leader as the new governor as well as various former rebels as mayors but also representatives of Indonesian political parties. Since this time, the former secessionist movement has ruled the province through the ballot box. Aceh has benefited from its longest period without armed conflict in recent memory. The enthusiasm for peace was clear, although qualified. As one man explained, "peace does not mean everything is final. War could return. But I want my grandson to go to school" (interview, March 2008).

What brought peace to Aceh? One could cite the destructive 2004 tsunami and subsequent global attention. It could be the 2005 Helsinki Memorandum of Understanding (MoU), in which foreign mediators helped convince Indonesian leaders and Acehnese rebels to end the war and accept autonomy. Finnish negotiator Martii Ahtisaari was awarded the 2008 Nobel Peace Prize in large part for his work in Aceh. It could be Indonesian democratization that allowed negotiations to be carried out in good faith. The new presidential team of Susilo Bambang Yudhoyono and Jusuf Kalla was elected months before the tsunami, initiating the talks that would lead to peace. Perhaps it was a "hurting stale-mate," with the rebels seeing little hope for successful independence as their movement waned (Zartman 2001). Or it could be the offer of genuine territorial autonomy, in which the rebels could run in elections and take the helm of a provincial government. Peace developed through all these factors and more. Peace is not a single document: it is a product of multiple phenomena and efforts, many of which do not make the headlines.

After several sections on armed conflict, this section lays out what has been done and what can still be done to overcome conflict and build peace. It also ties together the main themes of previous sections. As we have seen, different conflict types feature distinctive temporal trends. Revolutionary conflicts have largely been defeated, with their dramatic decline owed largely to international factors and more effective state responses. Secessionist insurgencies have also seen a downward trend, although it has not been as sharp and has occurred for different reasons, related more to peacebuilding efforts than global dynamics. Meanwhile, communal conflicts lack clear trends, representing an enduring threat to the peoples of Southeast Asia. These disparate threads tie back to the theme of ethnicity. The surviving conflicts are secessionist conflicts, which are rarely defeated and may recur, and communal conflicts, which can erupt at times of crisis. Both are varieties of ethnic conflict, with ethnic grievances and insecurities lingering long after violence occurs, available for local leaders and their communities to rekindle when the time is right. Ethnic conflicts must be managed, as part of an ongoing dialogue between majority and minority groups, rather than being resolved (Fisher 1993). This section shows how successful conflict management can involve ethnicity. Just as ethnicity can contribute to war, it can also shape peace through ethnic symbols, traditional leaders, reconciliation processes, and more. If armed conflicts in Southeast Asia are fueled by ethnic insecurities, then sustained peace demands that these are addressed.

5.1 Overcoming Revolutionary Conflicts

No Southeast Asian revolutionary conflict has been overcome through a high-level peace agreement. This is not for a lack of trying, with many cases of governments and insurgents coming to the table. Revolutionary insurgencies tend to resist compromise; unlike ethnic conflicts, revolutionaries seek to transform power at the center and target those holding power. When commun-ists demand overturning the socioeconomic system, those in power are unlikely to oblige. However, as discussed, Southeast Asian revolutionary conflicts are on the decline. For the most part, this is not due to peacebuilding or compromise but instead a result of international factors, government victories, and communist fragmentation – basically, defeating revolutionary insurgents. This does not mean, however, that peacebuilding efforts are irrelevant. And if communist grievances are not taken into account, there is a danger of recurrence or other forms of violence.

The most important structural factor in overcoming communist insurgencies was the end of the Cold War. Several Southeast Asian communist movements declined in the 1980s as the Soviet Union and China ceased supporting revolutionary governments and insurgencies. In Myanmar, the dramatic end to the communist conflict in 1989 "originated in the Chinese decision ten years earlier drastically to reduce aid to the CPB" (Lintner 1990, 39). Not only did China sever aid, but it also opened direct trade with the government and ethnic armies, further undermining CPB resources. The close of the Cold War severed aid for communists and diminished the allure of communism for recruits, weakening regional insurgencies.

Another international factor was the expansion of regional cooperation. This includes the growth of the Association of Southeast Asian Nations (ASEAN). Although ASEAN is often criticized for its inability to resolve armed conflicts (Caballero-Anthony 2005), the organization encourages communication among member countries, helping to reduce support for armed groups in neighboring countries and increase intelligence sharing (Kivimäki 2016). Cooperation between Thailand and Malaysia helped to overcome conflicts on both sides of the border. Despite originating as an anti-communist alliance, ASEAN later helped to normalize relations with Vietnam, Laos, and Cambodia. Vietnam's rapid economic reforms and growth in the 1990s were spurred in part by integration and membership in ASEAN, with the regional organization helping to socialize Vietnam and provide planning expertise.

Southeast Asian revolutionary conflicts thus declined in large part due to international factors, although domestic factors also played important roles. Southeast Asian governments pressed their advantages in the 1980s, securing military victories against communists. Many regional governments offered amnesties to encourage surrenders and promoted rural development to address grievances. Thomas (1986) explains that, after losing external assistance, the decline of communist insurgency in Thailand resulted from more effective government responses, including rural economic development and amnesty programs. Sebastian (1991) attributes the end of the CPM to Malaysia's improved ties with China and Thailand, government assaults, and the eventual decision to provide amnesties to remaining fighters in 1989. Even Myanmar's generals offered amnesties that enticed many communist recruits to lay down their arms and return home (Smith 2007, 35).

Another factor in the decline of revolutionary insurgency took place within communist movements, namely ethnic fragmentation. As we saw in Section 2, in Burma, Thailand, and Malaysia communists found recruits among specific ethnic communities. In light of the aforementioned pressures, divisions between leaders and followers became points of contention. The spectacular end of the CPB was a result of "ethnic mutinies" within the party, with ethnic minority recruits turning on leaders and refuting communist ideology as they reformed as an ethnic movement, the United Wa State Army (Smith 2007, 38). Southeast Asian communist movements always featured internal ethnic divisions; these fissures deepened with external pressure.

Social forces also diminished communist insurgencies. Many religious and traditional leaders had long opposed communist movements, as revolutionaries were often hostile to religion and worked to overturn societal hierarchies. Although sometimes sympathetic to communist demands, the overall opposition of religious and traditional leaders to communism was always a barrier to recruitment. Civil society groups have also confronted communist insurgencies, questioning their claims to represent the people. In response to the failure of government peace talks with communist insurgents, the Philippines saw the creation of the Coalition for Peace (CfP), a civil society movement that rejected violent conflict. Civil society organizations played a notable role in expanding the peace zone movement, in which civilians declare their communities to be "off limits" to combatants. Beginning in Naga City in southern Luzon, peace zones involved civil society, media, and church pressure on both sides to agree to respect the zones. Between 1988 and 1991, nine zones were created in areas that experienced significant clashes between state and communist forces (Avruch & Jose 2007). Because many religious, civil society, and ethnic leaders remained outside communist movements and the state, some groups were positioned to promote grassroots peace advocacy.

Overall, Southeast Asian revolutionary conflicts have declined as a result of international and domestic pressures. They have not ended as a result of compromise and systemic reform, as governments typically reject revolutionary demands and revolutionaries reject compromise. In the Philippines, the last Southeast Asian country with an active revolutionary insurgency, several peace talks have ended in disappointment. In 2012, talks with the CPP collapsed, as "the two parties could not even agree on the agenda," while the MILF "represented a more reliable negotiating partner" (Heydarian 2015, 4). The failure to overcome revolutionary conflict through compromise is disappointing, especially if this suggests that military victory is the only path. This said, revolutionary conflicts have also declined in part due to political reforms and economic development. It is not a coincidence that the Philippines, the lone country with an active communist insurgency, remains a perennial under-achiever in terms of development and equality, fueling revolutionary sentiment (Kusaka 2017, 91).

5.2 Overcoming Secessionist Conflicts

Unlike revolutionary insurgency, it is not uncommon for secessionism to be overcome through negotiation and compromise. Whereas governments and communists may not be able to find middle ground, governments and secessionists have been able to share power through territorial autonomy, allowing minorities self-government within existing borders. Although peace talks and autonomy agreements have not succeeded in all cases, and some conflicts are less suited to them than others, many conflicts have been overcome relatively peacefully. This is not, however, due solely to top-down negotiations, as grass-roots efforts reinforce high-level processes.

5.2.1 Peace Talks

In Aceh, peace talks were enabled by the presence of a fairly cohesive rebel movement and an increasingly democratic state. Shortly after the election of President Wahid in Autumn 1999, Indonesian authorities opened talks with GAM, mediated by the Centre for Humanitarian Dialogue, a Swiss NGO. This led to the 2000 Humanitarian Pause, a ceasefire which allowed for the delivery of aid to conflict victims for several months. Continued talks culminated in the December 2002 Cessation of Hostilities Agreement (CoHA). The CoHA involved international monitors, including an ASEAN contingent, and extended dialogues. However, as GAM refused to drop its demand for independence, the talks collapsed in May 2003, with Indonesia declaring a military emergency and attacking the rebels (Aspinall & Crouch 2003). These failed negotiations laid the groundwork for later talks. In late 2004, newly elected president Yudhoyono encouraged Vice President Jusuf Kalla to approach GAM. On December 26, a devastating tsunami struck the province, killing over 100,000 people. The tragedy accelerated peace talks, as international pressure and funding, a weary population, and a need to cooperate brought the two sides together. Mediated by former Finnish president Martti Ahtisaari, who learned from previous talks to address the fundamental issue of independence first, the result was the 2005 MoU (Aspinall 2005, 6). Success hinged on GAM's historic decision to renounce independence as well as the Indonesian compromise to allow the rebels to form a political party and contest elections. Built on previous peace talks, the Helsinki MoU helped to end a secessionist conflict.

Negotiations also helped overcome secessionism in Mindanao. The first process unfolded in 1976, with Libya mediating between Philippine president Marcos and the MNLF. The Tripoli Agreement saw rebels accept autonomy, but the conflict soon reignited. The failure demonstrates the challenges of negotiating with authoritarian leaders. President Marcos was personally involved in the talks, which he hoped would help relations with oil-exporting Muslim countries. Once the agreement was reached, Marcos shifted course, holding a questionable referendum that undermined autonomy. This deepened a split in the rebel movement and generated new forms of conflict. With Philippine democratization, officials held new talks with the MNLF in the late 1980s. An agreement was finally reached in 1996, as the MNLF agreed to demobilize and lead the Autonomous Region of Muslim Mindanao (ARMM). This did not resolve the conflict, as the MNLF periodically clashed with the government and the MILF continued its struggle (Bertrand 2000). In 2000, President Estrada attacked Moro rebels in an "all-out war" that destroyed MILF camps and displaced tens of thousands. After a series of Malaysian-mediated negotiations, which included expanded autonomy and attention to land rights, the MILF renounced independence and signed the 2014 Comprehensive Agreement on the Bangsamoro. This largely ended the secessionist struggle, even if it did not overcome other sources of violence in Mindanao (Loesch 2017).

Despite these successes, peace agreements may not work for all secessionist conflicts. Rebel group cohesion is essential in resolving violent conflicts through negotiations, as fragmented groups may include spoilers and be unable to follow through on their promises (Cunningham 2011, 294). As Staniland (2014, 3) observes, disciplined armed groups can control their ranks and limit violence, whereas "fractious groups and movements find themselves torn by patterns of outbidding and competitive violence between prospective leaders that make negotiations fall apart." For example, in Patani, violence is largely anonymous, consisting of terrorist attacks on public targets. For Helbardt (2015, 191), "Most perpetrators of insurgent violence remain anonymous, and hence supporters have a lack of knowledge about who is responsible." While organized, militants are not cohesive or public, with unclear demands or popularity. Nonetheless, Thai authorities have hosted peace talks on several occasions. In 2008, the military announced a ceasefire with various rebel groups, but this had no effect on violence, as the insurgents "had little or no control over activities on the ground" (McDermott 2013, 123). In 2015, the Thai government engaged in negotiations with a rebel consortium called MARA. The talks failed to make headway, "hindered by the militants' disunity" and doubt among observers whether rebel leaders "can speak for a critical mass of fighters" (ICG 2016). Rebel fragmentation does not make negotiations impossible or meaningless, but it is a considerable barrier. By extension, it is unclear if territorial autonomy, typically the objective of peace talks, would be as suitable for such cases, as there would be no popular group to lead a regional government.

5.2.2 Territorial Autonomy

Most peace negotiations with secessionist insurgents focus on creating territorial autonomy – ethnic minority self-government within existing national borders. It is even possible that scholars and policymakers place too much emphasis on peace talks, when it is the order such talks create that determines the long-term success of peace. Territorial autonomy is thus the most important tool for resolving and avoiding secessionist violence. It allows territorially concentrated minorities to govern their own affairs within the borders of a host country, meeting halfway between incorporation and independence. Self-government should be seen not just as a tool of conflict resolution but also as a tool of long-term conflict management. Territorial autonomy takes many forms, with regional government powers ranging from quasi-statehood to more symbolic concessions. Most autonomy arrangements stipulate control of resource revenue, local elections, and cultural policies.

The success of territorial autonomy depends on the degree to which autonomy is meaningful. Much depends on which powers are granted, as well as on how autonomy develops (whether it is given or negotiated) and who holds power (those loyal to the host state or leaders enjoying local legitimacy). This overview comes with a caveat: as with peace talks, autonomy may not be as effective where rebel groups and separatist regions lack cohesion (Mozaffar & Scarritt 1999). More unified secessionist regions are more amenable to governance by states or rebels; more fragmented regions offer less potential for peaceful order no matter who is in charge.

In Aceh, the promise of autonomy diminished the Darul Islam Rebellion in 1962. However, this promise was only partially implemented and then slowly was rescinded, something that fueled secessionism for many Acehnese (Miller 2008). As the secessionist conflict expanded, Indonesia reinstated Aceh's autonomy in 1999. This had little effect on the conflict. Amid peace talks with GAM, Indonesia gave Aceh even greater autonomy, with Nanggroe Aceh Darussalam (NAD) Law in January 2002. The NAD Law provided more substantive autonomy, allowing for traditional administrative divisions, a larger share of resource and taxation revenues, Islamic law, and more. Again though, autonomy had little effect on the conflict. Crucially, the NAD Law was given by Indonesian leaders, not negotiated with secessionists; it empowered pro-Jakarta Acehnese leaders and enabled new levels of corruption. As Miller (2004, 351) observes, Acehnese were immediately critical of the NAD Law, with the increased budget and local corruption "further alienating Acehnese society from the Indonesian state." In a sense, the NAD Law was an effort to undermine the rebels. Because of how it was granted and whom it empowered, it was immediately seen by many Acehnese as illegitimate, regardless of its contents. To be effective, territorial autonomy had to be negotiated, accompanied by a peace agreement, and include GAM. The Helsinki MoU led to what became the 2006 Law on Governing Aceh (LoGA). In substance, LoGA is not very different from the NAD Law (Aspinall 2014, 467). The biggest shift was local elections, with the former rebels running as independent executive candidates and forming a local political party. It was thus not just the substance of autonomy that mattered but how and to whom it was granted.

By contrast, autonomy in Papua essentially remains stalled, resembling Aceh in 2003–4. Faced with national turmoil in 1999, Indonesian leaders drafted autonomy arrangements for Papua, creating what would become known as Otsus (Otonomi Khusus, or Special Autonomy) with Law 21 of 2001. Papuan autonomy provides local control over resource revenue as well as significant transfer funds from Jakarta. It also created a special Papuan People's Assembly, a sort of legislature that parallels the provincial legislature, and instituted affirmative action for native Papuans. But like Aceh in 2003, Otsus in Papua is widely seen as illegitimate. As autonomy was granted, Indonesia carved out a new province called West Papua, thus violating their own autonomy agreement. At the same time, Indonesia cracked down on secessionism and protest. Because Otsus was given instead of negotiated, excluded rebel groups, and was accompanied by heavy-handed policies, it was widely criticized. Otsus funds enriched Papuan officials and deepened corruption, with governors marred by scandals. The failure of territorial autonomy is evident in protests, in which Papuan activists hold symbolic funerals for Otsus and ceremonially return it to Jakarta, as, for Bertrand (2010, 188), "Special Autonomy has failed to address the grievances of Papuans". Criticisms of autonomy were voiced by protesters in the 2019 Papuan riots, a marked statement of the failure of autonomy in Papua.

In Mindanao, some autonomy was granted by President Marcos after the Tripoli talks, and the Philippine government granted more substantial autonomy in 1989, creating the ARMM. Without a peace agreement and a change in government, though, autonomy failed to reduce conflict, instead fueling corruption among pro-Manila local leaders. This changed in 1996 when a peace agreement enabled MNLF leaders to take power through the ARMM, resolving part of the conflict. Mindanao remained at war, however, as the MILF remained active and the ARMM government was ineffective. For Quimpo (2001, 276), peace talks "promised genuine autonomy for Muslims in Mindanao," but the outcome was disappointing, as "few Muslims appear to be satisfied with the actual results." Rood (2012, 274) suggests that this was in large part due to rebel fragmentation and the "particularistic clan-based power structure of traditional politics." After an agreement with the MILF, the ARMM was formally superseded by the Bangsamoro Autonomous Region in Muslim Mindanao in 2019. The Mindanao conflict is not entirely resolved, with ongoing talks regarding the scope of autonomy, but peace talks with autonomy have in large part overcome secessionism.

Just as the conflict-resolving powers of territorial autonomy are significant, provided that autonomy accompanies a peace agreement and includes former rebels, territorial power-sharing can also help prevent secessionist conflict (Cederman et al. 2015). It seems that federalism and autonomy have helped to avoid conflict in Malaysia, even if the national government has slowly usurped state power. In the north, Kelantan and Terengganu border Patani, a region known for its strong Islamic identity and distinctive Malay culture. The Malaysian side of the border has not seen secessionism, perhaps because states have been able to chart their own course, ruled in large part by the Malaysian Islamic Party (PAS). Other non-cases are the eastern Malaysian states of Sabah and Sarawak. These autonomous states feature unique political party systems, controls on internal migration, and special recognition of indigenous peoples. Autonomy in Sabah and Sarawak has corroded over time but has nonetheless helped to diminish secessionist sentiment and avoid secessionist conflict.

Recognizing the ethnic dimensions of revolutionary insurgencies suggests that some cases could benefit from autonomy. Many communist insurgencies have flourished among hill peoples, whose grievances were translated through a class lens. The CPB found support among Myanmar's ethnic minorities, groups which later rebelled against the party and transformed themselves into ethno-secessionist groups. In Thailand, communists were especially powerful in Isan, which has a distinctive pan-Lao ethnic identity. In the 1960s, Keyes (1967) referred to regionalist sentiment and rebellion here as "the Isan problem," one that would continue into the future unless Thailand provided more effective local governance. Today, Isan remains an impoverished, distinctive region in Thailand and supports the Red Shirt protests against elites in Bangkok. It is possible that some form of autonomy might mitigate regional tensions.

5.2.3 Grassroots Activism

Thus far, this discussion has focused on top-down approaches, namely peace negotiations and territorial autonomy. Secessionist conflicts have also diminished as a result of more grassroots efforts. The Zones of Peace movement that developed in the Philippine communist insurgency also spread to Mindanao, where religious, media, and NGO leaders worked with villagers to make their homes off-limits to both sides. Neither state nor rebel forces wanted to agree to peace zones, but both sides were concerned about their reputations and did not want to be seen to reject them if the other side agreed (Hancock & Mitchell 2007). Another example from Mindanao is "Bakwit Power," where IDPs rallied to encourage peace and criticized both sides for destructive violence (Canuday 2009). Civil society organizations have also helped combatants maintain ceasefires. One such local organization, Bantay Ceasefire, utilizes social media and SMS messaging from locals, dispatching monitoring teams when tensions escalate and investigation teams after clashes. In one example, the MILF was accused of violating the ceasefire, something the rebels denied. Bantay Ceasefire discovered that a feud between an uncle and his nephew over a personal matter became violent and drew in some rebels. Technically, MILF fighters violated the ceasefire, but it was for personal matters and against orders. The MILF accepted blame and the ceasefire was sustained (Colletta 2006).

Peacebuilders increasingly acknowledge the importance of traditional, cultural mechanisms of responding to armed conflict. The value of such traditional institutions is that, if they are cultural norms, they can unfold across many villages without formal coordination, their higher-level importance felt in aggregation through thousands of smaller efforts. Traditional systems have many shortcomings, as they tend to be dominated by conservative male elders, and it is often unclear how they align with official peacebuilding processes. Regardless, traditional systems of justice often enjoy local legitimacy, demanding greater appreciation by scholars and policymakers. They show how ethnic traditions can help build peace, especially by promoting mediation and reconciliation.

In Aceh, villages have reintegrated former combatants and IDPs by adapting a traditional ceremony called the *peusijuek*. Literally meaning "to cool off," the *peusijuek* developed for youths who had gone abroad for faith, study, or profit, recognizing that their return could be disruptive. The ceremony involves communal prayers, sprinkling holy water, and feasting. They can be massive, multiday festivals or smaller, more intimate affairs. After the Aceh conflict, traditionalist Islamic leaders adapted the *peusijuek* for peacebuilding, doing so without formal coordination (Barter 2019). *Peusijuek* have helped to reintegrate former rebel commanders, acknowledging their victims and offering apologies, as well as IDPs. The ceremony thus helped to demobilize and reintegrate combatants as well as conflict IDPs, contributing to rebuilding communities.

The involvement of Islamic leaders, who provided their blessings and led oaths that forbade further violence, was especially important. Such traditional ceremonies have limitations, though, as provincial ethnic minorities have been excluded from ceremonies seen as ethnically Acehnese. Traditional ceremonies may thus require supervision and complementary efforts to ensure inclusion.

Although several secessionist conflicts stubbornly resist resolution, many have diminished through peace efforts. More than revolutionary insurgencies, secessionist insurgencies are amenable to compromise, with peace negotiations helping to develop systems of meaningful self-government through territorial autonomy. Meanwhile, grassroots peacebuilding can challenge combatants, push them to negotiate, and sustain peace. Ethnic conflicts demand conflict management. For conflicts involving territorially concentrated minorities, self-government represents a valuable approach, especially when accompanied by community-based peace mechanisms. Such grassroots efforts are especially important in overcoming Southeast Asia's many communal conflicts.

5.3 Managing Communal Conflicts

Communal conflicts are exceptionally difficult to resolve. Here, rivals are neighboring communities, their interspersion making self-government unlikely and potential clashes difficult to avoid. The fact that combatants are often also ordinary people, not highly organized armed groups, also makes resolution difficult. Managing communal conflicts demands diffuse approaches to peace that take ethnic traditions and insecurities seriously.

Although communal conflicts are intergroup, the state is always involved in shaping violence. In insurgencies, when the state establishes order by force, this represents state victory and rebel defeat. In communal conflicts, there is more room for the state to step in to halt violence and punish those responsible, establishing order to stop violence. For Horowitz (2001), the most effective long-term way to prevent riots is state-building: creating an effective state that can channel group interests and establish a neutral, professional police presence. States can also control precipitants of violence such as marches and incendiary speeches, as well as develop a more inclusive socioeconomic system.

One example of preventing communal conflicts is found in southern Sumatra. The province of Lampung has seen extensive migration, with native Lampungese representing a minority alongside Javanese transmigrants. This is a likely case for ethnic tensions and migratory conflict. But Lampung has remained peaceful, which Côté (2019) attributes partly to traditional ceremonies such as *mawori*, in which migrants are symbolically adopted into the Lampungese community and families, including being given Lampungese names. This "fictive kinship" helps integrate the Javanese, providing symbolic respect to native Lampung culture. Where conflicts have arisen, *mawori* have helped to manage disputes. This said, traditional ceremonies have limitations. Côté notes that *mawori* have been less effective in managing tensions with Balinese Hindu migrants. Again, traditional ceremonies may have limits in terms of who can participate, tempering our expectations of their effectiveness.

Overcoming violent communal conflicts may involve peace talks, although such talks are different than those found in insurgencies. After communal violence, peace talks typically include representatives from militant groups and state authorities, but they can also involve traditional and religious leaders as well as representatives of the broader society. Whereas peace agreements in insurgencies feature leaders with the capacity to negotiate and enforce agreements, in communal conflicts peace processes are more symbolic and inclusive. Ceremonies might involve oaths against violence, an emphasis on shared traditions, spiritual endorsements of peace, forgiveness ceremonies, and the creation of monitoring groups.

Held in eastern Indonesia to diminish conflict between Christian and Muslim communities, the Malino Accords exemplify more inclusive communal peace processes. The process began in Sulawesi, the site of destructive Christian–Muslim conflicts. In 2001, Indonesian government officials organized meetings in South Sulawesi involving various groups. The quasi-official talks created bodies to manage security, help IDPs, and provide counseling. It also mobilized Muslim and Christian leaders, as well as *adat* (traditional) leaders, to encourage peace, provide reassurances, and emphasize common bonds. Events included peace prayers, gift exchanges, and communal feasting. This model inspired similar processes in Maluku. The Malino II Declaration involved similar ceremonies and led to the demobilization and arrest of Islamic militias, as well as the creation of joint investigation teams. Malino II supported the creation of interfaith organizations, including the Team of 20 in Wayame village and Provokator Perdamaian (Peace Provocateurs), whose activities included organizing oaths of loyalty between specific churches and mosques, as well as forbidding derogatory religious slang (al Qurtuby 2013). In both cases, it is not that subsequent acts of communal violence were absent but instead that local communities handled future incidents constructively to quarantine violence. The success of the Malino system led to suggestions that other communal conflicts in Southeast Asia could benefit from similar quasi-state traditional ceremonies (ICG 2012).

In communal conflict, ethnic insecurities and religious differences can generate significant violence, especially as they are fanned by rumors. As a result, effective community responses to communal conflict involve addressing insecurities, emphasizing shared beliefs, creating incentives for elites to promote peace, and monitoring violence and rumors. Bubant (2008) has shown that rumors in the form of photocopied pamphlets helped to expand communal violence in Maluku, deepening insecurities and fueling paranoia. Emerging from American race riots in the 1960s, many regions with a history of communal conflict have created rumor control centers (Young, Pinkerton & Dodds 2014). The local councils established by the Malino Accords have taken up the task of controlling rumors, seeking to verify information and challenge provocative misinformation (Rohman & Ang 2019). Rumor control has taken on a new urgency given social media, with state agencies and journalists playing important roles in quelling unsubstantiated rumors.

Preventing communal conflicts requires ensuring that communities feel respected and included. Where several ethnic communities coexist peacefully, designing political institutions around ethnicity may heighten ethnic differences. But where ethnic violence has already surfaced and remains salient, political systems must accommodate ethnic differences. This might include guaranteed group representation at varied levels of government and forms of affirmative action. Borrowing elements from consociationalism, in which democratic competition is dulled in favor of cooperation between ethnic elites (Lijphart 1969), can help promote minority inclusion and group representation. In Singapore and Malaysia, we see what Mauzy (2013) dubs "coercive consociationalism." Singapore has seen various efforts to improve minority representation, evident in reserving the largely symbolic presidency for minorities, various electoral innovations, housing policies limiting ethnic concentrations, and multicultural policies more generally (Kymlicka & He 2005). Different approaches are found in Malaysia. One of the keys to the long-standing dominance of the Barisan Nasional was that the ruling coalition always included non-Malays. Notably, when the ruling coalition was finally unseated in 2018, the opposition movement was also a multiethnic coalition. Malaysian politics demand coalition politics and group representation. In Myanmar, the legislative upper house (the House of Nationalities) is intended partly to represent ethnic groups, and in 2011 the country introduced two vice-president posts, which in 2016 enabled the appointment of the first-ever Christian vice president.

Other consociational measures are smaller-scale and informal. Indonesian elections often feature mixed tickets in legislative and executive contests. Presidential races are often contested by president/vice president pairs representing Java and the Outer Islands, as well as nationalist and Islamic parties, in an effort to gain votes that also entails an element of inclusion. In subnational elections, electoral rules and campaign strategies encourage cross-ethnic pairs, a mechanism aimed at electoral gain that also sustains peace. In post-conflict Maluku, elections have seen Christian and Muslim running mates. In 2008, for example, all four gubernatorial candidate pairs consisted of a Muslim and a Christian, connecting different political parties as well as different Maluku subregions. For Tomsa (2009, 247), "in a political environment in which balance between Christians and Muslims was perceived to be paramount, all four candidates had no choice but to choose running mates from 'the other' religion, whether they liked it or not." Returning to Lampung, the traditional *mawori* ceremony of Javanese being adopted into native Lampungese culture extends to elections, with ethnic Javanese taking Lampung names when running for office and typically including native running mates (Côté 2019). Such power-sharing norms help bring communities together across Indonesia, providing rivals with representation and reassurances.

5.4 Conclusions

This section focused on how to move toward peace in three types of armed conflict in Southeast Asia. It emphasized that, despite some commonalities, each type of conflict involves distinct challenges and trends. Communist insurgencies have not been resolved through high-level negotiations and compromise but instead through the weakening of communist movements due to international factors, domestic reforms, and internal divisions. Although a form of insurgency, secessionist conflicts have proven more amenable to compromise, as power sharing through territorial autonomy represents a middle ground between independence and incorporation. In both forms of insurgency, we should also pay attention to grassroots peace work, including civil society efforts to challenge combatants, as well as efforts to reintegrate and reconcile conflict-torn societies. These grassroots approaches are especially important in managing communal conflicts. Although state-led peace talks can also be useful in dealing with such conflicts, they depend in large part on the efforts of numerous actors, organizations, and traditions.

6 Conclusions

Southeast Asia has endured a variety of violent armed conflicts. Revolutionary, secessionist, and communal conflicts have cost hundreds of thousands of lives, injured and displaced millions, undermined human and economic development, deepened ethnic tensions, and more. As this Element has demonstrated, armed conflicts in Southeast Asia have declined, although forms of ethnic conflict – especially communal conflicts – continue to haunt many countries in the region.

This study sought to make four broad contributions: to provide a useful typology of conflict types; to draw attention to the importance of ethnicity in shaping conflict dynamics; to highlight broader trends in the rise and decline of armed conflicts; and to better understand approaches to conflict resolution and management. This final section summarizes each contribution then looks ahead to the future of war and peace in Southeast Asia.

Understanding armed conflict requires recognizing different types of conflict, along with areas of overlap. Revolutionary, secessionist, and communal conflicts present distinctive challenges, varying in their causes, timing, armed groups, goals, patterns of violence, external allies, approaches to peace, and more. Revolutionary and secessionist conflicts are insurgencies, fought by armed rebel groups against the state, while communal conflicts feature less cohesive combatants and different state roles. Secessionist and communal conflicts, meanwhile, are forms of ethnic conflict, driven by ethnic symbols and insecurities, although revolutionary conflicts also contain important ethnic dimensions. Although these conflicts differ in important ways, they also overlap, connected as types of insurgencies and ethnic conflicts. Revolutionary insurgencies involve ethnicity, but ethnic conflicts also involve class dimensions, often being inspired by communist movements and focusing on the exploitation of their peoples and territories. All three types of conflict feature varied outcomes and subtypes. Crucially, revolutionary and secessionist insurgencies vary in their patterns of resolution, with revolutionary conflicts more likely to end in rebel defeat and some secessionist conflicts ending in compromise.

This Element stressed the importance of ethnicity in shaping all forms of armed conflict in Southeast Asia. In this diverse world region, ethnicity has informed the organization, goals, and actions of armed groups. This is true even for revolutionary movements, which at first glance may appear unrelated to ethnicity but feature nationalist themes, ethnic symbols and recruitment, ethnic divisions, and ethnically defined opposition. For example, communist insurgents in Malaysia recruited mostly from ethnic Chinese, while in Indonesia communists were disproportionately Javanese. In Myanmar and Thailand, communist parties featured sharp internal ethnic divides, shaping choices of external allies and the parties' eventual collapse. Secessionist and communal conflicts present even clearer roles for ethnicity, with armed groups couching goals and grievances in terms of group identity. In secessionist and communal conflicts, leaders often stoke ethnic insecurities and exaggerate ethnic differences, sometimes attacking local minorities. Emphasizing how ethnicity shapes violent conflicts may lead some to see ethnicity as inherently dangerous and as a problem to be solved. In a sense, studies of violent conflicts are guilty of selecting on the dependent variable, homing in on the relatively rare but important instances of conflict. Ethnic violence is relatively uncommon, even in Southeast Asia, with communities being enriched rather than imperiled by difference. Ethnic traditions can also encourage peace, as explained in Section 5.

This study presented important macro-level trends in regional conflict dynamics. Based on data collected by PRIO as well as other sources, it is clear that different types of conflict feature distinctive trajectories in the region. A comparison of conflict trends uncovers varying levels of intensity. At their height, Southeast Asian revolutionary conflicts killed approximately 25,000–45,000 people per year, with secessionist conflicts peaking at around 8,000–12,000 casualties and communal conflicts spiking through various pogroms, from time to time killing thousands. Revolutionary insurgencies were thus most deadly, explained in part by the external aid they received, the direct threat they posed to central governments, and their potential to be waged across an entire country. Secessionist insurgencies, by contrast, are less likely to receive external assistance and are confined to specific territories. They have been deadlier than most communal conflicts, though, since they are more likely to be sustained, fought by insurgent armies in remote regions. Communal conflicts tend to explode in brief flares of violence, escalating into pogroms where states refuse to restore order and tacitly support killings.

Overall, Southeast Asia has seen a decline in conflict-related deaths. This outcome is consistent with global trends. The number and intensity of wars are declining, even if we might think otherwise based on media reports. Pinker (2012, xxiv) finds that, since World War II, "the great powers, and developed states in general, have stopped waging war on one another." Wars within states have also become less common: "since the end of the Cold War in 1989, organized conflicts of all kinds – civil wars, genocides, repression by autocratic governments, and terrorist attacks – have declined throughout the world." Similarly, Goldstein (2011) argues that "*Interstate* wars have become very infrequent and relatively small ... The number of *civil wars* is also shrinking, though less dramatically, as old ones end faster than new ones begin" (emphasis in original). Even with more recent conflicts in Syria and ongoing violence in Iraq and Sudan, armed conflicts have declined around the world. This is true in Southeast Asia, where armed conflicts are being overcome, or at least managed, and the total number of active conflicts and their human toll declining.

Although declining in aggregate, different types of armed conflicts demonstrate distinctive trajectories. Revolutionary insurgencies were the deadliest form of conflict, then declined drastically at the end of the 1970s through the 1980s, responsible only for several hundred deaths per year in Southeast Asia by the 2000s. Secessionist insurgencies exhibited a downward trend in casualties in the 2000s but were still responsible for approximately a thousand deaths per year in the 2010s. Communal conflicts, however, show no broad arc, with no clear reduction over time. Communal conflicts are the most numerous but also the smallest-scale form of conflict in Southeast Asia. The intensity of riots, pogroms, and migratory conflicts spikes in moments of political crisis; these are constant threats that should not be ignored amid a broader decline in regional armed conflicts.

Despite decreasing regional violence, the continued threat posed by ethnic conflicts demands that we continue to consider varied approaches to peacebuilding and long-term conflict management. Section 5 explained the decline in communist conflict as being largely due to international factors, namely the end of the Cold War and dwindling external support for insurgencies. Revolutionary movements saw external pressures amplify internal ethnic divisions, leading to the defeat of rebel groups. Understanding the ethnic dimensions of these conflicts is important for grasping post-conflict dynamics, as the former communist stronghold of Isan in Thailand sees continued unrest and former communist forces in Myanmar have reorganized into ethnic armies. Revolutionary insurgencies continue today, especially in the Philippines, and the effects of revolutionary insurgencies are still felt throughout the region.

Secessionist conflicts have declined in their intensity. Some have largely been overcome through peace agreements, allowing self-government through territorial autonomy. But in Papua, Patani, and several regions in Myanmar, secessionist violence continues. Secessionist insurgencies have not disappeared as completely as revolutionary insurgencies, and they tend to reemerge if states mismanage delicate ethnic power relations. When we consider communal conflicts, it is clear that ethnic conflicts remain enduring threats in Southeast Asia, suggesting the need for expansive approaches to peace. Instead of resolution, it is important to approach ethnic conflicts in terms of long-term conflict management. This is at the heart of the success of territorial autonomy, which creates new systems of minority self-government. Managing ethnic conflicts must involve a wide range of actors and symbols, providing reassurances and healing along with ongoing communication. In Western countries, scholars observe how majorities tend to speak of resolving historical injustices, whereas indigenous and other minorities dealing with historical grievances speak of ongoing dialogues, trust-building, and healing (Lightfoot 2015). For ethnic conflicts, there is unlikely to be a single moment of resolving past injustices, as feelings of resentment and fear run deep. Instead, managing ethnic conflicts demands a long-term, inclusive vision that respectfully incorporates ethnic leaders and traditions.

Although we are not out of the woods yet, armed conflicts in Southeast Asia, even communal conflicts, are being resolved and managed. To demonstrate, we return to Sulawesi in Indonesia, home to a communal conflict between Christians and Muslims. The presence of peace does not, sadly, mean the absence of violence. In 2005, militants beheaded three Christian schoolgirls in an effort to reignite communal violence. The result, however, was not widespread riots and retributive violence. Christian communities were outraged, but so were Muslims. Islamic leaders spoke out against the militants and supported their Christian neighbors. The attackers were soon captured and given lengthy jail sentences, avoiding the death penalty only after a tearful act of forgiveness by the victims' families. One of the girls' mothers emphasized that the attacks must not reignite violence in Poso: "they won't be able to provoke us, we don't want another war. We want justice, not vengeance" (Guardian 2005). In the wake of horrific violence in a conflict-prone region, the test for peace is not the absence of violence but instead handling its presence. Despite – and because of – tragic conflict, the affected communities in Poso demonstrated a desire to maintain peace. Such examples suggest that a more peaceful Southeast Asia is possible, perhaps even likely.

Glossary

AA Arakan Army

ALA Arakan Liberation Army

ARMM Autonomous Region of Muslim Mindanao

ASEAN Association of Southeast Asian Nations

ASG Abu Sayyaf Group

BGF Border Guard Forces

BRN Barisan Revolusi Nasional (National Revolutionary Front)

CAVR Comissão de Acolhimento, Verdade e Reconciliação (Commission for Reception, Truth and Reconciliation)

COW Correlates of War

CCPT Chinese Communist Party of Thailand

CPB Communist Party of Burma

CPP Communist Party of the Philippines

CPT Communist Party of Thailand

CPV Communist Party of Vietnam

Fretilin Frente Revolucionária de Timor-Leste Independente (Revolutionary Front for an Independent East Timor)

GAM Gerakan Aceh Merdeka (Free Aceh Movement)

HRW Human Rights Watch

ICP Indochinese Communist Party

IDP internally displaced person

KIO Kachin Independence Organization

KNPP Karenni National Progressive Party

KNU Karen National Union

LoGA Law on Governing Aceh

MCP Malayan Communist Party

MILF Moro Islamic Liberation Front

MNLF Moro National Liberation Front

MoU Memorandum of Understanding

NAD Nanggroe Aceh Darussalam

NMSP New Mon State Party

NPA New People's Army

OPM Organisasi Papua Merdeka (Free Papua Movement)

PKI Partai Komunis Indonesia (Indonesian Communist Party)

PRIO Peace Research Institute Oslo

PULO Patani United Liberation Organization

RMS Republik Maluku Selatan (Republic of South Maluku)

SSA Shan State Army

SSNA Shan State National Army

UN United Nations

References

Abinales, P. (2000). *Making Mindanao: Cotabato and Davao in the Formation of the Philippine Nation-State*. Manila: Ateneo University Press.

Adam, J. (2013). "A Comparative Analysis on the Micro-Level Genealogies of Conflict in the Philippines' Mindanao Island and Indonesia's Ambon Island." *Oxford Development Studies* 41(2): 155–72.

al Qurtuby, S. (2013). "Peacebuilding in Indonesia: Christian–Muslim Alliances in Ambon Island." *Islam and Christian-Muslim Relations* 24(3): 349–67.

Aljunied, S. M. K., and R. A. Curaming (2012). "Mediating Violence and Consuming Memories of Violence: The Jabidah Massacre in the Philippines." *Critical Asian Studies* 44(2): 227–50.

Anderson, B. (1991). *Imagined Communities: Reflections on the Origin and Spread of Nationalism*. London: Verso.

(1993). "Imagining 'East Timor.'" *Arena Magazine* 4: 23–7.

Aragon, L. V. (2001). "Communal Violence in Poso, Central Sulawesi: Where People Eat Fish and Fish East People." *Indonesia* 72(2): 45–79.

Arcilla, G. (2019). "NICA Chief Says CPP-NPA Wants Power, not Peace." *Philippine News Agency*, June 20.

Arjona, A., N. Kasfir, and Z. Mampilly, eds. (2015). *Rebel Governance in Civil War*. Cambridge: Cambridge University Press.

Aspinall, E. (2005). *The Helsinki Agreement: A More Promising Basis for Peace in Aceh?* Honolulu: East–West Center Policy Studies 20.

(2009). *Islam and Nation: Separatist Rebellion in Aceh, Indonesia*. Stanford, CA: Stanford University Press.

(2014). "Special Autonomy, Predatory Peace, and the Resolution of the Aceh Conflict." In *Regional Dynamics in a Decentralized Indonesia*, ed. H. Hill, 460–81. Singapore: ISEAS.

Aspinall, E., and H. Crouch (2003). *The Aceh Peace Process: Why It Failed*. Honolulu, HI: East–West Center Policy Studies 1.

Avruch, K., and R. S. Jose (2007). "Peace Zones in the Philippines." In *Zones of Peace*, ed. L. E. Hancock and C. Mitchell, 51–70. Bloomfield, CT: Kumarian.

Barter, S. J. (2013). "State Proxy or Security Dilemma? Understanding Anti-rebel Militias in Civil War." *Asian Security* 9(2): 75–92.

(2015a). "Second-Order Minorities in Asian Secessionist Conflicts." *Asian Ethnicity* 16(2): 123–35.

(2015b). "Between a Rock and a Hard Place: Second-Order Minorities in the Aceh Conflict." *Asian Ethnicity* 16(2): 152–65.

(2018). "Rethinking Territorial Autonomy." *Regional Studies* 52(2): 298–309.

(2019). "Displacement and Reintegration in Aceh, Indonesia." In *Internal Migration: Challenges in Governance and Integration*, ed. S. J. Barter and W. A. Ascher, 113–28. New York: Peter Lang.

Barter, S. J., and I. Côté (2015). "Strife of the Soil? Unsettling Transmigrant Conflicts in Indonesia." *Journal of Southeast Asian Studies* 46(1): 60–85.

Barter, S. J., and W. A. Ascher, eds. (2019). *Internal Migration: Challenges in Governance and Integration*. London: Peter Lang.

Bartholomew-Feis, D. R. (2006). *The OSS and Ho Chi Minh: Unexpected Allies in the War Against Japan*. Lawrence: University of Kansas Press.

Bertrand, J. (2000). "Peace and Conflict in the Southern Philippines: Why the 1996 Peace Agreement is Fragile." *Asian Survey* 73(1): 37–54.

(2004). *Nationalism and Ethnic Conflict in Indonesia*. Cambridge: Cambridge University Press.

(2010). "The Double-Edged Sword of Autonomy in Indonesia and the Philippines." In *Multinational States in Asia: Accommodation or Resistance*, ed. J. Bertrand and A. Laliberté. Cambridge: Cambridge University Press, 164–195.

Bertrand, J., and A. Pelletier (2017). "Violent Monks in Myanmar: Scapegoating and the Contest for Power." *Nationalism and Ethnic Politics* 23(3): 257–279.

Brancati, D. (2006). "Decentralization: Fueling the Fire or Dampening the Flames of Ethnic Conflict and Secessionism?" *International Organization* 60(3): 651–685.

Brass, P., ed. (1996). *Riots and Pogroms*. Albany: New York University Press.

Brubaker, R., and D. Laitin (1998). "Ethnic and Nationalist Violence." *Annual Review of Sociology* 24(1): 423–452.

Bubant, N. (2008). "Rumors, Pamphlets, and the Politics of Paranoia in Indonesia." *Journal of Asian Studies* 67(3): 789–817.

Buchanan, J. (2017). *Militias in Myanmar*. San Francisco: The Asia Foundation.

Caballero-Anthony, M. (2005). *Regional Security in Southeast Asia: Beyond the ASEAN Way*. Singapore: Institute of Southeast Asian Studies.

Canuday, J. J. (2009). *Bakwit: The Power of the Displaced*. Manila: Ateneo de Manila University Press.

Capuno, J. J. (2019). "Probing Conflict Contagion and Casualties in Mindanao, Philippines." *Defence and Peace Economics*: 1–20.

Carey, P. (1999). "The Catholic Church, Religious Revival, and the Nationalist Movement in East Timor, 1975–98." *Indonesia and the Malay World* 27(78): 77–95.

CAVR (Comissão de Acolhimento, Verdade e Reconciliação) (2005). *Chega! Report of the Commission for Reception, Truth and Reconciliation in East Timor.* Dili: Government of East Timor.

Cederman, L. E. (2002). "Nationalism and Ethnicity." In *Handbook of International Relations*, ed. W. Carlsnaes, T. Risse, and B. Simmons, 409–28. London: Sage.

Cederman, L. E., N. Weidmann, and K. S. Gleditsch (2011). "Horizontal Inequalities and Ethnonationalist Civil War: A Global Comparison." *American Political Science Review* 105(3): 478–95.

Cederman, L. E., S. Hug, A. Schädel, and J. Wucherpfenning (2015). "Territorial Autonomy in the Shadow of Conflict: Too Little, Too Late?" *American Political Science Review* 109(2): 354–70.

Chandler, D. P. (1991). *The Tragedy of Cambodian History: Politics, War, and Revolution since 1945.* New Haven, CT: Yale University Press.

Chandra, K., ed. (2012). *Constructivist Theories of Ethnic Politics.* Oxford: Oxford University Press.

Chang, P. M. (1982). "The Sino-Vietnamese Dispute over the Ethnic Chinese." *China Quarterly* 90: 195–230.

Cheng, A. L. H. (2001). "The Past in the Present: Memories of the 1964 'Racial Riots' in Singapore." *Asian Journal of Social Science* 29(3): 431–55.

Chirot, D., and A. Reid (2011). *Essential Outsiders: Chinese and Jews in the Modern Transformation of Southeast Asia and Central Europe.* Seattle: University of Washington Press.

Christie, C. (2001). *Ideology and Revolution in Southeast Asia, 1800–1980: Political Ideas of the Anti-colonial Era.* London: Curzon Press.

Clutterbuck, R. (1985). *Conflict and Violence in Singapore and Malaysia 1945–1983.* London: Westview.

Coakley, J. (1993). "Introduction: The Territorial Management of Ethnic Conflict." *Regional Politics and Policy* 3(1): 1–22.

Colletta, N. J. (2006). "Citizen Security – the Role of NGOs and Broader Civil Society in Ceasefire Monitoring: Lessons from Mindanao." *Journal of Peacebuilding and Development* 2(3): 21–34.

Côté, I. (2019). "Adopting Migrants as Brothers and Sisters – Fictive Kinship as a Mechanism of Conflict Resolution and Conflict Prevention in Lampung, Indonesia." In *Internal Migration: Challenges in Governance and Integration*, ed. S. J. Barter and W. A. Ascher, 97–112. New York: Peter Lang.

Côté, I., and L. E Huang (2020). "Where are the Daughters? Examining the Effects of Gendered Migration on the Dynamics of 'Sons of the Soil' Conflict." *Studies in Conflict and Terrorism*.

Côté, I., and M. I. Mitchell (2017). "Deciphering 'Sons of the Soil' Conflicts: A Critical Survey of the Literature." *Ethnopolitics* 16(4): 333–51.

Cribb, R. (2001). "Genocide in Indonesia, 1965–1966." *Journal of Genocide Research* 3(2): 219–39.

Crocombe, R. (2007). *Asia in the Pacific Islands: Replacing the West*. Fiji: University of the South Pacific.

Cunningham, K. G. (2011). "Divide and Conquer or Divide and Concede: How Do States Respond to Internally Divided Separatists?" *American Political Science Review* 105(2): 275–97.

Davidson, J. S. (2008). *From Rebellion to Riots: Collective Violence on Indonesian Borneo*. Madison: University of Wisconsin Press.

di Tiro, H. (1979). *The Drama of Achehnese History, 1873–1978*. State of Acheh: Self-published.

(1984). *The Price of Freedoms: The Unfinished Diary of Tengku Hasan di Tiro*. State of Acheh: Self-published.

DSW (Deep South Watch) (2019). "DSW Database." https://deepsouthwatch.org.

Eck, K. (2009). "From Armed Conflict to War: Ethnic Mobilization and Conflict Intensification." *International Studies Quarterly* 53(2): 369–88.

Egreteau, R. (2011). "Burmese Indians in Contemporary Burma: Heritage, Influence, and Perceptions since 1988." *Asian Ethnicity* 12(1): 33–54.

Ehrentraut, S. (2011). "Perpetually Temporary: Citizenship and Ethnic Vietnamese in Cambodia." *Ethnic and Racial Studies* 34(5): 779–98.

Elfversson, E., and J. Brosché (2012). "Communal Conflict, Connections, and the Case of Sudan." *African Journal on Conflict Resolution* 12(1): 9–32.

Fan, H. (2012). "The 1967 Anti-Chinese Riots in Burma and Sino-Burmese Relations." *Journal of Southeast Asian Studies* 43(2): 234–56.

Fearon, J. D. (2004). "Separatist Wars, Partition, and World Order." *Security Studies* 13(4): 394–415.

Fearon, J. D., and D. D. Laitin (2003). "Ethnicity, Insurgency, and Civil War." *American Political Science Review* 97(1): 75–90.

Fisher, R. J. (1993). "The Potential for Peacebuilding: Forging a Bridge from Peacekeeping to Peacemaking." *Peace & Change* 18(3): 247–66.

Fox, J. (2004). "The Rise of Religious Nationalism and Conflict: Ethnic Conflict and Revolutionary Wars, 1945–2001." *Journal of Peace Research* 41(6): 715–31.

Goldstein, J. S. (2011). *Winning the War on War: The Decline of Armed Conflict Worldwide*. London: Penguin.

Goscha, C. E. (2003). "Revolutionizing the Indochinese Past: Communist Vietnam's 'Special Historiography' on Laos." In *Contesting Visions of the Lao Past: Laos Historiography at a Crossroads*, ed. C. E. Goscha and S. Ivarsson, 265–300. Copenhagen: NIAS Press.

Guan, A. C. (2018). *Southeast Asia's Cold War: An Interpretive History*. Honolulu: University of Hawaii Press.

Guardian (2005). "Machete Killings Fuel Indonesia's Religious Hatred." November 19, 2005.

Guterres, A. (2018). "UN Secretary General Press Remarks". www.un.org/sg/en/content/sg/press-encounter/2018–07-02/transcript-secretary-general%E2%80%99s-remarks-press-encounter.

Hancock, L., and C. Mitchell, ed. (2007). *Zones of Peace*. London: Kumarian Press.

Hamilton-Merritt, J. (1993). *Tragic Mountains: The Hmong, the Americans, and the Secret War for Laos, 1942–1992*. Bloomington: Indiana University Press.

Harish, S. P. (2006). "Ethnic or Religious Cleavage? Investigating the Nature of the Conflict in Southern Thailand." *Contemporary Southeast Asia* 28(1): 48–69.

Hawkins, M. C. (2013). *Making Moros: Imperial Historicism and American Rule in the Philippine's Muslim South*. Dekalb: Northern Illinois Press.

Helbardt, S. (2015). *Deciphering Southern Thailand's Violence: Organization and Insurgent Practices of BRN-Coordinate*. Singapore: ISEAS.

Henley, D. E. (1995). "Ethnogeographic Integration and Inclusion in Anti-colonial Nationalism: Indonesia and Indochina." *Comparative Studies in Society and History* 37(2): 286–324.

Heydarian, R. J. (2015). "The Quest for Peace: The Aquino Administration's Peace Negotiations with the MILF and CPP-NPA-NDF." Norwegian Peacebuilding Resource Centre Report.

Ho Chi Minh (1945). "Proclamation of Independence of the Democratic Republic of Vietnam."

Holmes, R. A. (1967). "Burmese Domestic Policy: The Politics of Burmanization." *Asian Survey* 7(3): 188–97.

Horowitz, D. (1985). *Ethnic Groups in Conflict*. Berkeley: University of California Press.

(2001). *The Deadly Ethnic Riot*. Berkeley: University of California Press.

HRW (Human Rights Watch) (1997). "Indonesia: Communal Violence in West Kalimantan."

(2002). "Indonesia: Four Years of Communal Violence in Central Sulawesi."

ICG (2016). "Southern Thailand's Peace Dialogue: No Traction." Briefing 148, September 21, 2016.

(2012). "What Could Myanmar Learn from Indonesia? The Malino Accord."

Kalyvas, S. N. (2006). *The Logic of Violence in Civil War.* Cambridge: Cambridge University Press.

Kalyvas, S. N., and M. A. Kocher (2007). "Ethnic Cleavages and Irregular War: Iraq and Vietnam." *Politics & Society* 35(2): 183–223.

Kammen, D. (2003). "Master–Slave, Traitor–Nationalist, Opportunist–Oppressed: Political Metaphors in East Timor." *Indonesia* 76: 69–85.

Kaplow, J. M. (2016). "The Negotiation Calculus: Why Parties to Civil Conflict Refuse to Talk." *International Studies Quarterly* 60(1): 38–46.

Kaufman, S. J. (2001). *Modern Hatreds: The Symbolic Politics of Ethnic War.* Ithaca, NY: Cornell University Press.

(2011). "Symbols, Frames, and Violence: Studying Ethnic War in the Philippines." *International Studies Quarterly* 55(4): 937–58.

Kaufmann, C. (1996). "Intervention in Ethnic and Ideological Civil Wars: Why One Can Be Done and the Other Can't." *Security Studies* 6(1): 62–101.

Kell, T. (1995). *The Roots of Acehnese Rebellion, 1989–1992.* Ithaca, NY: Cornell University Press.

Kerkvliet, B. J. (1977). *The Huk Rebellion: A Study of Peasant Revolt in the Philippines.* Berkeley: University of California Press.

Keyes, C. F. (1967). "Isan: Regionalism Regional in Northern Thailand." Cornell Thailand Series, Data Paper 66.

Kiernan, B. (2002). *The Pol Pot Regime: Race, Power, and Genocide in Cambodia under the Khmer Rouge, 1975–79.* New Haven: Yale University Press.

King, D. Y., and M. R. Rasjid (1988). "The Golkar Landslide in the 1987 Indonesian Elections: The Case of Aceh." *Asian Survey* 28(9): 916–25.

Kivimäki, T. (2016). *The Long Peace of East Asia.* London: Routledge.

KKR (Komisi Kebenaran dan Rekonsiliasi Aceh) (2019). "Aceh Truth and Reconciliation Commission: A Diplomatic Brief." Available at http://kkr-aceh.com.

Krause, J. (2020). "Restrained or Constrained? Elections, Communal conflicts, and Variation in Sexual Violence." *Journal of Peace Research* 57(1): 185–98.

Kusaka, W. (2017). *Moral Politics in the Philippines: Inequality, Democracy, and the Urban Poor.* Singapore: NUS Press.

Kymlicka, W., and B. He (2005). *Multiculturalism in Asia.* Oxford: Oxford University Press.

Lev, D. S. (1967). "Political Parties in Indonesia." *Journal of Southeast Asian History* 8(1): 52–67.

Levitsky, S., and L. Way (2013). "The Durability of Revolutionary Regimes." *Journal of Democracy* 24(3): 5–17.

Lightfoot, S. (2015). "Settler-State Apologies to Indigenous Peoples: A Normative Framework and Comparative Assessment." *Native American and Indigenous Studies* 2(1): 15–39.

Lijphart, A. (1969). "Consociationalism Democracy." *World Politics* 21(2): 207–25.

Lintner, B. (1990). *The Rise and Fall of the Communist Party of Burma*. Ithaca, NY: SEAP Publications.

Loesch, J. (2017). "The GPH–MILF Peace Process in the Philippines to Prevent and Transform Violent Extremism in Mindanao." *Journal of Peacebuilding and Development* 12(2): 96–101.

Luong, H. V. (1992). *Revolution in the Village: Tradition and Transformation in North Vietnam, 1925–1988*. Honolulu: University of Hawaii Press.

Lyall, Jason, and Isaiah Wilson III (2009). "Rage against the Machines: Explaining Outcomes in Counterinsurgency Wars." *International Organization* 63(1): 67–106.

Magno, J. P. and A. Gregor (1986). "Insurgency and Counterinsurgency in the Philippines." *Asian Survey* 26(5): 501–17.

Mampilly, Z. C. (2012). *Rebel Rulers: Insurgent Governance and Civilian Life During War*. Ithaca, NY: Cornell University Press.

Marx, K. (1844). *A Critique of Hegel's Philosophy of Right*.

Marx, K., and F. Engels. (1848). *Manifesto of the Communist Party*.

Mason, T. D., J. P. Weingarten, and P. J. Fett (1999). "Win, Lose, or Draw: Predicting the Outcome of Civil Wars." *Political Research Quarterly* 52(2): 239–68.

Mauzy, D. K. (2013). "Malaysia: Malay Political Hegemony and 'Coercive Consociationalism'." In *The Politics of Ethnic Conflict Regulation: Case Studies of Protracted Ethnic Conflicts*, ed. J. McGarry and B. O'Leary, 118–39. London: Routledge.

Mauzy, D. K., and R. S. Milne (2002). *Singapore Politics Under the People's Action Party*. London: Routledge.

McCargo, D. (2008). *Tearing the Land Apart: Islam and Legitimacy in Southern Thailand*. Ithaca, NY: Cornell University Press.

McCarthy, J. F. (2007). "The Demonstration Effect: Natural Resources, Ethnonationalism, and the Aceh Conflict." *Singapore Journal of Tropical Geography* 28(3): 314–33.

McCoy, A., ed. (2009). *An Anarchy of Families: State and Family in the Philippines*. Madison: University of Wisconsin Press.

McDermott, G. B. (2013). "Barriers toward Peace in Southern Thailand." *Peace Review* 25(1): 120–128.

McKenna, T. M. (1998). *Muslim Rulers and Rebels: Everyday Politics and Armed Separatism in the Southern Philippines*. Berkeley: University of California Press.

McVey, R. (2006). *The Rise of Indonesian Communism*. Jakarta: Equinox Publishing.

Miller, M. A. (2004). "The Nanggroe Aceh Darussalam Law: A Serious Response to Acehnese Separatism?" *Asian Ethnicity* 5(3): 333–51.

(2008). *Rebellion and Reform in Indonesia: Jakarta's Security and Autonomy Policies in Aceh*. London: Routledge.

Mozaffar, S., and J. R. Scarritt (1999). "Why Territorial Autonomy Is Not a Viable Option for Managing Ethnic Conflict in African Plural Societies." *Nationalism and Ethnic Politics* 5(3–4): 230–53.

MSF (Médecins Sans Frontièrs) (2017). "Rohingya Refugee Crisis." www .msf.org/myanmarbangladesh-msf-surveys-estimate-least-6700-rohingya -were-killed-during-attacks-myanmar.

Nathan, K. S. (1990). "Malaysia in 1989: Communists End Armed Struggle." *Asian Survey* 30(2): 210–20.

Paredes, O. (1997). "Higaûnon Resistance and Ethnic Politics in Northern Mindanao." *Australian Journal of Anthropology* 8(3): 270–90.

(2015). "Indigenous vs. Native: Negotiating the Place of Lumads in the Bangsamoro Homeland." *Asian Ethnicity* 16(2): 166–85.

Penders, C. L. M. (2002). *The West New Guinea Debacle: Dutch Decolonization and Indonesia, 1945–1962*. Honolulu: University of Hawaii Press.

Pinker, S. (2012). *The Better Angels of Our Nature: Why Violence Has Declined*. New York: Penguin Books.

Pouvatchy, J. R. (1986). "Cambodian-Vietnamese Relations." *Asian Survey* 26(4): 440–51.

PRIO (Peace Research Institute Oslo) (2012). "PRIO Battle Deaths Dataset 3.1." B. Lacina and N. P. Gleditsch.

Pye, L. (1956). *Guerrilla Communism in Malaysia*. Princeton: Princeton University Press.

Quimpo, N.G. (2001). "Options in the Pursuit of a Just, Comprehensive, and Stable Peace in the Southern Philippines." *Asian Survey* 41(2): 271–289.

Race, J. (1973). *War Comes to Long An: Revolutionary Conflict in a Vietnamese Province*. Berkeley: University of California Press.

Rahimmula, C. (2003). "Peace Resolution: A Case Study of Separatist and Terrorist Movement in Southern Border Provinces of Thailand." *Songkhlanakarin Journal of Social Science and Humanities* 10(1): 98–112.

Reid, A. (2005). *An Indonesian Frontier: Acehnese and Other Histories of Sumatra*. Singapore: National University of Singapore Press.

Reilly, B. (2008). "Ethnic Conflict in Papua New Guinea." *Asia Pacific Viewpoint* 49(1): 12–22.

Ricklefs, M. C. (2012). *Islamicisation and Its Opponents in Java: A Political, Social, Cultural, and Religious History, c. 1930 to the Present*. Singapore: NUS Press.

Riwanto, T. (2013). *From Colonization to Nation-State: The Political Demography of Indonesia*. Jakarta: LIPI Press.

Robinson, G. (2009). *"If You Leave Us Here, We Will Die": How Genocide Was Stopped in East Timor*. Princeton, NJ: Princeton University Press.

   (2018). *The Killing Season: A History of the Indonesian Massacres, 1965–66*. Princeton, NJ: Princeton University Press.

Rohman, A., and P. H. Ang (2019). "Truth, not Fear: Countering False Information in a Conflict." *International Journal of Communication* 13: 4586–601.

Rood, S. (2012). "Interlocking Autonomy: Manila and Muslim Mindanao." In *Autonomy and Armed Separatism in South and Southeast Asia*, ed. M.A. Miller, 256–77. Singapore: ISEAS.

Sambanis, N. (2001). "Do Ethnic and Nonethnic Civil Wars Have the Same Causes? A Theoretical and Empirical Inquiry." *Journal of Conflict Resolution* 45(3): 259–82.

Sanford, S. (2019). "Myanmar's Karen Rebel Groups Reunite for Anniversary." VOA News.

Sarkees, M. R., and F. Wayman (2010). "COW War Data, 1816–2007." Washington DC: CQ Press.

Scott, J. S. (2009). *The Art of Not Being Governed: An Anarchist History of Upland Southeast Asia*. New Haven, CT: Yale University Press.

Sebastian, L. (1991). "Ending an Armed Struggle without Surrender: The Demise of the Communist Party of Malaya (1979–89) and the Aftermath." *Contemporary Southeast Asia* 13(3): 271–98.

Short, A. (1970). "Communism, Race, and Politics in Malaysia." *Asian Survey* 10(12): 1081–9.

Sidel, J. T. (2006). *Riots, Pogroms, Jihad: Religious Violence in Indonesia*. Ithaca, NY: Cornell University Press.

Siegel, James T. (1998). "Early Thoughts on the Violence of May 13 and 14, 1998 in Jakarta." *Indonesia* 66: 75–108.

Simbulan, R. G. (2016). "Indigenous Communities' Resistance to Corporate Mining in the Philippines." *Peace Review* 28(1): 29–37.

Sison, J. M. (2004). *Jose Maria Sison: At Home in the World, Portrait of a Revolutionary*. London: Open Hand Publishing.

Sjamsuddin, N. (1985). *The Republic Revolt: A Study of the Acehnese Rebellion*. Singapore: ISEAS.

Smith, A. D. (1979). "Towards a Theory of Ethnic Separatism." *Ethnic and Racial Studies* 2(1): 21–37.

    (1996). "Culture, Community, and Territory: The Politics of Ethnicity and Nationalism." *International Affairs* 72(3): 445–68.

Smith, M. (2007). *State of Strife: The Dynamics of Ethnic Conflict in Burma*. Honolulu: East-West Center Policy Studies 36.

Solahudin (2013). *The Roots of Terrorism in Indonesia: From Darul Islam to Jem'ah Islamiyah*. Ithaca, NY: Cornell University Press.

Somers-Heidhues, M. (2012). "Anti-Chinese Violence in Java during the Indonesian Revolution, 1945–49." *Journal of Genocide Studies* 14(3–4): 381–401.

St. John, R. B. (2006). *Revolution, Reform, and Regionalism in Southeast Asia: Cambodia, Laos, and Vietnam*. London: Routledge.

Staniland, P. (2014). *Networks of Rebellion: Explaining Insurgent Cohesion and Collapse*. Ithaca, NY: Cornell University Press.

Stark, J. (2003). "Muslims in the Philippines." *Journal of Muslim Minority Affairs* 23(1): 195–209.

Stuart-Fox, M. (1979). "Factors Influencing Relations between the Communist Parties of Thailand and Laos." *Asian Survey* 19(4): 333–52.

Taras, R., and R. Ganguly (2015). *Understanding Ethnic Conflict*. London: Routledge.

Taylor, R. H. (1983). "The Burmese Communist Movement and Its Indian Connection: Formation and Factionalism." *Journal of Southeast Asian Studies* 14(1): 95–108.

Temby, Q. (2010). "Imagining an Islamic State in Indonesia: From Darul Islam to Jemaah Islamiyah." *Indonesia* 89: 1–36.

Thawnghmung, A. M. (2012). *The 'Other' Karen in Myanmar: Ethnic Minorities and the Struggle without Arms*. New York: Lexington Books.

Thomas, M. L. (1986). "Communist Insurgency in Thailand: Factors Contributing to its Decline." *Asian Affairs* 13(1): 17–26.

Tomsa, D. (2009). "Electoral Democracy in a Divided Society." *South East Asia Research* 17(2): 229–59.

Topmiller, R. (2002). *The Lotus Unleashed: The Buddhist Peace Movement in South Vietnam, 1964–66*. Lexington: University Press of Kentucky.

Torres, W. M. (2014). *Rido: Clan Feuding and Conflict Management in Mindanao*. Manila: Ateneo de Manila University Press.

UN (United Nations) (1948). Convention on the Prevention and Punishment of the Crime of Genocide.

UNHCR (UN High Commissioner for Refugees) (2019). "UN Independent International Fact-Finding Mission on Myanmar Calls on UN Member States to Remain Vigilant in the Face of the Continued Threat of Genocide." New York: October 23, 2019.

van der Kroef, J. M. (1981). *Communism and South-East Asia*. London: MacMillan Higher Education.

Viartasiwi, N. (2018). "The Politics of History in West Papua – Indonesia Conflict." *Asian Journal of Political Science* 26(1): 141–59.

Vu, T. (2016). *Vietnam's Communist Revolution: The Power and Limits of Ideology*. Cambridge: Cambridge University Press.

Walton, M. J., and S. Hayward (2014). *Contesting Buddhist Narratives: Democratization, Nationalism, and Communal Violence in Myanmar*. Honolulu: East-West Center Policy Studies 71.

Weiner, M. (1978). *Sons of the Soil: Migration and Ethnic Conflict in India*. Princeton, NJ: Princeton University Press.

Weiss, M. (2020). "Legacies of the Cold War in Malaysia: Anything but Communism." *Journal of Contemporary Asia* 50(4): 511–29.

Wood, J. R. (1981). "Secession: A Comparative Analytical Framework." *Canadian Journal of Political Science* 14(1): 107–34.

Young, S., A. Pinkerton, and K. Dodds (2014). "The Word on the Street: Rumor, Race, and the Anticipation of Urban Unrest." *Political Geography* 38: 57–67.

Zartman, I. W. (2001). "The Timing of Peace Initiatives: Hurting Stalemates and Ripe Moments." *Global Review of Ethnopolitics* 1(1): 8–18.

Acknowledgments

The author would like to thank the Centre for Asia-Pacific Initiatives at the University of Victoria as well as the Indonesia Project and Department for Social and Political Change at Australian National University, which hosted me during my sabbatical from Soka University of America. This sabbatical was supported by Soka's Pacific Basin Research Center. This project benefited from the support of several research assistants, including Kennah Watts, Thuy Le, Muskan Agrawal, Mahesh Kushwaha, and Kelsey Castanho, as well as input from Jamie Davidson. Series editors Edward Aspinall and Meredith Weiss, along with three anonymous reviewers, provided considerable feedback and criticisms – thank you! Finally, I would like to thank my long-time mentor Diane Mauzy, who hopefully finds the echoes of her teaching in these pages.

Politics and Society in Southeast Asia

Edward Aspinall
Australian National University
Edward Aspinall is a professor of politics at the Coral Bell School of Asia-Pacific Affairs, Australian National University. A specialist of Southeast Asia, especially Indonesia, much of his research has focused on democratisation, ethnic politics and civil society in Indonesia and, most recently, clientelism across Southeast Asia.

Meredith L. Weiss
University at Albany, SUNY
Meredith L. Weiss is Professor of Political Science at the University at Albany, SUNY. Her research addresses political mobilization and contention, the politics of identity and development, and electoral politics in Southeast Asia, with particular focus on Malaysia and Singapore.

About the Series
The Elements series Politics and Society in Southeast Asia includes both country-specific and thematic studies on one of the world's most dynamic regions. Each title, written by a leading scholar of that country or theme, combines a succinct, comprehensive, up-to-date overview of debates in the scholarly literature with original analysis and a clear argument.

Cambridge Elements $\overline{\overline{}}$

Politics and Society in Southeast Asia

A full series listing is available at: www.cambridge.org/ESEA

Printed in the United States
By Bookmasters